My Life in Carnoustie

Robert Murray

Other Books by Robert Murray

The Grocer's Boy:
A Slice of His Life in 1950s Scotland

The Grocer's Boy Rides Again:
Another Slice of His Life in 1960s Scotland and Beyond

The Grocer's Boy Gets Down to Business:
The End Slice of His Career from the Easy-Going Seventies
to the Ultra-Competitive Nineties

The Spirit of Robbie Burns

MY LIFE IN CARNOUSTIE

A Lang Time Ago

Robert Murray

My Life in Carnoustie: A Lang Time Ago by Robert Murray.

First edition published in Great Britain in 2025 by Extremis Publishing Ltd., Suite 218, Castle House, 1 Baker Street, Stirling, FK8 1AL, United Kingdom.

www.extremispublishing.com

Extremis Publishing is a Private Limited Company registered in Scotland (SC509983) whose Registered Office is Suite 218, Castle House, 1 Baker Street, Stirling, FK8 1AL, United Kingdom.

Copyright © Robert Murray, 2025.

Robert Murray has asserted the moral right under the Copyright, Designs and Patents Act 1988 to be identified as the author of this work.

The views expressed in this work are solely those of the author, and do not necessarily reflect those of the publisher. The publisher hereby disclaims any responsibility for them.

This book is a work of non-fiction. Unless otherwise noted, the authors and the publisher make no explicit guarantees as to the accuracy of the information included in this book and, in some cases, the names of people, places and organisations may have been altered to protect their privacy. All hyperlinks were believed to be live and correctly detailed at the time of publication.

This book may include references to organisations, feature films, television programmes, popular songs, musical bands, novels, reference books, and other creative works, the titles of which are trademarks and/or registered trademarks, and which are the intellectual properties of their respective copyright holders.

All rights reserved. No part of this publication may be reproduced, stored in a retrieval system, or transmitted, in any form or by any means, electronic, mechanical, photocopying, recording or otherwise, without the prior permission in writing of the publisher.

This book is sold subject to the condition that it shall not, by way of trade or otherwise, be lent, re-sold or hired out, or otherwise circulated without the publisher's prior consent in any form of binding or cover other than that in which it is published and without a similar condition including this condition being imposed on the subsequent purchaser.

A CIP catalogue record for this book is available from the British Library.

ISBN: 978-1-0682314-1-4

Typeset in Sorts Mill Goudy, designed by The League of Moveable Type.

Printed and bound in Great Britain by IngramSpark, Chapter House, Pitfield, Kiln Farm, Milton Keynes, MK11 3LW, United Kingdom.

Cover design and book design is Copyright © Thomas A. Christie.

Author images are Copyright © Julie Christie and Eleanor Jewson.

Archive photography is sourced from the authors' private collections unless otherwise stated.
The copyrights of third parties are reserved. All third party imagery is used under the provision of Fair Use for the purposes of commentary and criticism. While every reasonable effort has been made to contact copyright holders and secure permission for all images reproduced in this work, we offer apologies for any instances in which this was not possible and for any inadvertent omissions.

Contents

Introduction..Page 1
1. My Childhood.. Page 9
2. High Days and Holidays.. Page 37
3. Carnoustie... Page 65
4. Faith and Religion...Page 109
5. My Family..Page 123
6. My Early Working Life... Page 145
7. Motoring.. Page 155
8. A Few More Thoughts..Page 165

Acknowledgements...Page 194
Notes on Front Cover Artwork..Page 195
About the Author..Page 196

A 1970s bus outing in Shamrock Street, Carnoustie.

MY LIFE IN CARNOUSTIE

Robert Murray

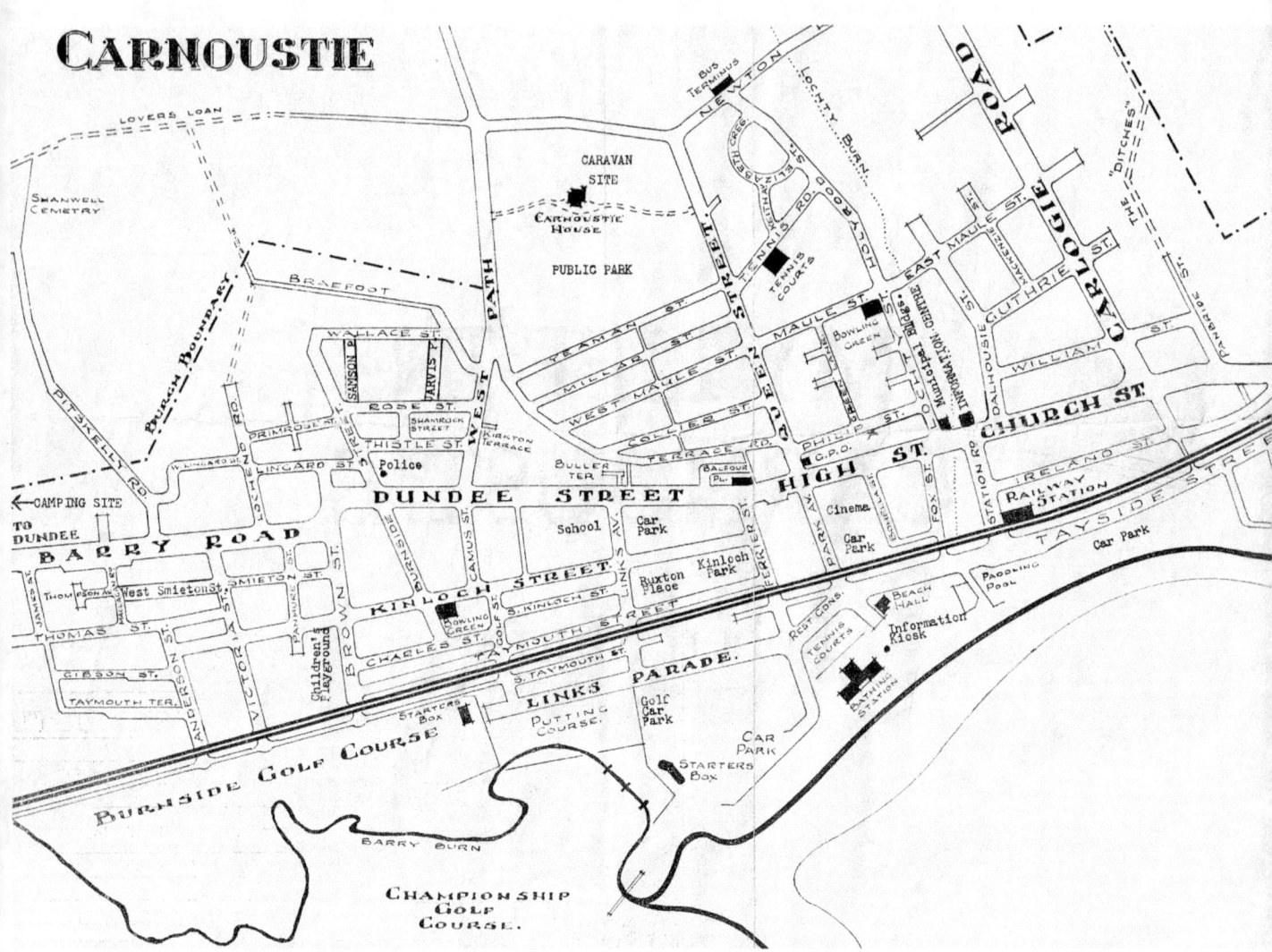

1950s Street Map of Carnoustie

Introduction

Having read several publications about the history of Carnoustie, I have never found a personal account which reflects day to day life of a past period.

There is nothing special about my life, but I am interested in the history of the town and its heritage. I merely want to leave some record of what life was like.

This is not meant to be only about me and my family, although I use my stories to convey social history of the time, so yes —I am a Carnoustie heritage addict.

Heritage is an "evergreen" subject: every generation has its own stories to leave behind.

Prompted and inspired by seeing on the "Auld Carnoustie" Facebook Group the many interesting snippets and photos relating to the town, I feel the need to put together a collection of my own family memories along with a more general view of Carnoustie during the days when I grew up in the town.

The area around Carnoustie has a long history, while my part in it is very small indeed. Hence, in 2025, I look back to my early days of growing up in the town—for me, "a lang time ago", or, in the true context of time, "just a wee while ago."

My thanks to the many well-known local names and photos which help to illustrate my story.

I owe so much to Carnoustie, my hometown, and from a heritage point of view I merely want to leave a record of one person's life in the town. My hope is that others, in the town will find ways to record and publish their own stories.

There are many families in Carnoustie today whose ancestors lived in the area, and I love to hear their tales and see their pictures. My parents, on the other hand, were "incomers" to the town in 1939.

Born in 1940 at Barry, my snippets relate to Carnoustie from the 1940s onwards. Later, "life and work" took me off to "foreign" parts, until I returned around the year 2000 to help my brother James (Peem) look after our mum, Bella Murray, until she passed away in April 2015 just three months after her 100th birthday.

weavers". Some men aspired to be a Grieve (farm manager). In the case of my father's family background, by sheer good fortune of geographic location, they found themselves—in Victorian times—employment on the London/Aberdeen mainline or railway tracks in the county. I have some excellent examples of copperplate handwritten letters written by both grandfathers reflecting on their early life and indicating an excellent early schooling.

It took me many years in my youth to realise there was no lack of intelligence on the part

Family Origins

My family tree takes me back to the year 1663, to areas in Angus on the coast as well as those deep in the county such as Guthrie, Dunnichen, Menmuir, Tigerton, Balnamoon, and Little Brechin—where families on each side of my parents lived and worked on the land. Yes, they were all farm workers—or as described by some, "teuchters"—hard-working farm labourers eking out a living by also working as "linen hand loom

My mother's parents, George and Annie (nee Hutcheson) Taylor, at the door of Dunninald Croft, near Montrose.

of diligent country folk—it was the lack of opportunity which defined their future. One of my uncles, born in 1904, left a farm bothy at the age of 19 to join the Aberdeen city police force, eventually rising to become Chief Inspector in the CID. Another example was his mother, my granny, who advised the builder of a new pigsty to incorporate a sluice in the wall at knee height, thus avoiding her lifting a heavy bucket of pigswill up to chest height and leaning over to drop the contents. Yes, farm labourers, but clever people. Of course, what they lacked in their poverty and cramped living conditions (four in a bed, top to toe) was outweighed by the plentiful supply of high quality, free local food of the countryside. Gruelling hard work governed by the seasons and long dark winters—no wonder many Scots from lowly origins became inventors!

Some years ago, I met with James Hutcheson—formerly producer of many Arbroath minstrel shows. His grandfather and my granny were brother and sister, and I

My grandfather, George Taylor, at work on Boddin Farm, near Lunan Bay.

can't help thinking that our shared interest in music, drama and stage work may have been handed down from our shared ancestors who played, sang and recited early day "bothy nicht" material.

As mentioned, my history began at Barry. Mum, Isabella Taylor, grew up at Boddin, near Montrose, where her father was Grieve on Boddin Farm. She met and married Bob Murray, then living at Lunan Bay. In her schooldays, Mum walked three miles to Craig School near Montrose, then spent her working life as maid/cook at Dunninald

Castle. Before working on the railway, Dad was employed by Chivers, the Cambridge-based jam company, and helped look after the raspberry crop grown all around the Montrose area.

Mum, the seventh child of a seventh child, was born with an energy and brightness, and was a deceptively good 'reader' of people. Dad had four siblings and was a calm, quiet man, and took all mum's ideas, plans and ambitions in his stride. They grew up only three miles apart—yet, because of their respective employments, they met only in their early twenties.

Mum and dad celebrated their 25th birthdays on the 3rd and 6th December 1939 respectively, and three days later they were married at Craig Church, near Montrose; a time for brief family celebrations amid the concerns of war.

Four generations: My great grandfather Mr Edwards (Lunan Smiddy's Master Blacksmith), my father Bob Murray, Baby Robbie Murray, and my granny Mary Murray (nee Edwards).

Dad had applied for a job with the London Midland and Southern (LMS) Railway Company, to be based at nearby Usan, but was unsuccessful and accepted an alternative offer as railway "signalman/ porter" at Monifieth, then immediately moved to 89 Brook Street in the town.

Later, when posted to a similar job at Barry, near Carnoustie, mum and dad rented rooms in the bungalow (next door to Barry School) where I was born in 1940. I was baptised at Craig Church, near Montrose, by the Rev. Mr P. S. Bisset. The following year, James (Peem), my brother, was born in the same house at Barry and was baptised at Barry (East) Church.

Peem went to Art College in Dundee, and became a professional artist with D.C.

My mother, Bella Taylor (right), worked as a maid at Dunninald Castle.

Thomson. He latterly engaged in newspaper computer page planning. On taking early retirement, he enjoyed two more careers—caddying for golfers from all over the world on Carnoustie's Championship Course, and working as part-time barman. To this day he keeps his artistic skills finely tuned, creating oil paintings of cats and dogs.

Our family moved to Annfield Cottages, Barry Road, Carnoustie around 1942, and my sister Isobel was born there in July 1944. She became a senior secretary, near Carlisle, for Lord Carlisle. Sadly, Isobel suffered a lung problem and died at Little Corby, near Carlisle, on 4th November 2008 aged only 64—incredibly sad, untimely, and a huge loss in our family.

In 1947, the year of a serious snowstorm, we moved to 4 Anchor Place, Admiral Street in Westhaven, where we enjoyed a gloriously happy period of around eight years. Our wee sister Jean was born in November 1953, and luckily the following year a three-bedroomed semi-detached council property at 4 Shamrock Street, Carnoustie became our family home, where mum continued to live until her 99th year in 2014. She then moved to a cottage within Kinloch Care Centre, in the town. Jean would later follow her big sister into the secretarial world as a medical secretary in Ayrshire.

Consequently, with my family history outlined above, it follows that my parents were relative newcomers to Carnoustie. Having said that, they happily "adopted" the town and made numerous close friends. They enjoyed the network of people and organisations, and found the town a pleasant place. This must have offered a greater social scene than the quiet rural countryside around Boddin Farm. My father died aged 85 on 5th February 2000, and my mother—still with bright and cheery alertness— suffered a collapse caused by pneumonia and passed away on 27th April 2015 in her 101st year.

We enjoyed such loving and caring parents, and my brother, my sisters and I all had a wonderful young life growing up in Carnoustie.

My father, Bob Murray (right), a Chivers raspberry farm worker.

Carnoustie: Some Background

Recently, when referring to "Friends of Carnoustie and District Heritage"—an organisation which encourages delving into the history of the town—a friend of mine remarked, "Heritage, Robbie? There's nae history in this toon." How wrong he was!

Although, in the 16th century, golf was being played on the grass areas around the marram-covered dunes surrounding the Barry Burn, it was not until the 1840s when the first "course" was laid out.

Prior to 1797, the area surrounding Carnoustie was a large farm in the Parish of Barry, and as early as 1573 a Mr Fairney was paying Arbroath Abbey for two feus in the area near Barry. As time passed, successive generations of families owned the land, and in 1792 Major William Philips—having purchased the large area for £5,000—set out with a friend, David Hunter of Pitskelly, to conceive the idea of building a village they called Taymouth Feus. In 1798, the first feu was taken up by a Barry loom wright, Tammas Lousen, who became known as the "founder" of the town.

In 1807 Major Philips sold the 'village' (the area of feus) to George Kinloch for £11,000, who named it Carnoustie and designed a grid of streets. He encouraged tradespeople to settle and set up in business.

Despite some theories that the rookeries on the high trees north of the town gave rise to the name "Craw's Nestie," it is more likely that Carnoustie's name came from ancient Pictish language for "Hill of the Fir Trees".

The story of Panbride and its parish church goes back even further—to the 11th Century, along with the origins of East Haven and Westhaven. Linda Nicoll, a local historian and author, has written a detailed history of Panbride Parish church.

Salmon fishing, crofting, and milling were occupations from the earliest of times, followed by a period of flax production and the associated cottage industry of spinning and weaving. As the industrial period evolved, linen factories were developed, followed by foundries. Early small-scale shoe-making enterprises developed into a substantial shoe factory. Gradually, the town became wholly self-sufficient, providing employment for all—supported by a bustling retail and commercial sector. Carnoustie's reputation as a desirable holiday resort began in the late 19th century and grew to a peak up to the mid-1950s, until inexpensive package holidays to Europe lured holiday-makers away.

Robbie's last day at school in July 1955.
From L to R: Back Row: Norma Mirrey, May Whyte, Mr Ian Currie (Maths Teacher), Mr Donald (English Teacher). Middle Row: Margot Gordon, Sandy McCauley, John Robb, John Blair, John Ferrier, Willie Yool. Front Row: Jean Adamson, Margaret Ross, Jim Fairweather, Richard Simmons, Robbie Murray (holding his Baby Kodak camera).

CHAPTER 1
My Childhood

Schools

"Remember to put your slate and bottle of water in your schoolbag!"

Barry School was a primary school for children aged 5 to 12 years living in the village of Barry and its surrounding area—including children living at Barry Road, Carnoustie.

I attended Barry School for my first primary school year while my family lived at Annfield Cottages, Barry Road, prior to moving to Admiral Street, Westhaven. I then attended the primary school which was part of Carnoustie Junior Secondary School (established in 1907), located at the west corner of Links Avenue and Dundee Street.

Panbride School was able to operate on the same basis as Barry school and recruited from Easthaven, Scryne and Muirdrum. Barry and Panbride schools are now (at 2025) closed. The school building at Barry is now converted into business units, while the building at Panbride is used occasionally by special social groups.

My memories at Barry School are deeply etched—in particular, during winter, sitting close to a roasting fire protected by a large metal fireguard. Miss Bell was my teacher, and I recall the quite horrible school lunches and always being last to finish my food. "Come on, Robert Murray! You are last to finish again!" I heard every day. I suspect I picked my way slowly through my unsavoury food.

Equally memorable were very wet days when I seemed to be the only pupil walking to school from Barry Road. The road between my home and school was tricky because floods covered the road and pavement, forcing me to "tiptoe" my way along the top of the high grassy kerb. I recall my shoes and socks being dried out quite often on Miss Bell's fireguard.

I can still recall commencing my primary school year at Carnoustie. It was the immediate post-Second World War period, and prominent memories included the slate (in a wooden frame) on which we wrote and did arithmetic. We took a bottle of water and a cloth to school each day to clean our slate. Occasionally, we were issued with a piece of toilet paper upon which we did our "special writing"—what luxury!

My primary school years were very happy and constructive, with quite strict lady teachers such as Miss Murray (with long strands of raffia hanging inside her cupboard door) and Miss Allison, and eventually in Primary 6 with Ronnie Brown (who told adventure and

Extreme left is the original Carnoustie Public school of 1907.
In the centre section is the art, technical and science block.
On the right is the extended section built in 1954.
My class was one of the first to occupy that part.

ghostly stories) followed by the severe and effective Mr McHutcheon ("Hutchie") in the "Qualifying" (Qualie) year. He shook us all up (by which I mean wakened us up "mentally") with ten mental arithmetic fraction "calculations" first thing every morning. It was during the "Qualie" year that we learned Robert Burns poetry. We were given a test by having to write out Burns' poems, complete with perfect spelling, every exclamation mark, full stop, and in Burns' exact words. I tied in top place with a girl

A ten-year-old Robbie Murray on his way home from school. In the background is Peem, followed by Oliver (Ollie) Scott of Westhaven Coastguards.

(Elizabeth Paul), and because her writing was 'prettier' than mine she was awarded the Burns trophy. I was hurt but what could I say? But there was a more damning policy in the "qualie" year (or 11+ year).

I should add at this point that the whole point of a "qualifying year" was to determine which pupils would be accepted to advance to Arbroath High School to follow a higher education course leading to Scottish education Ordinary ("O") Grade certificates and Higher Grade ("Highers") certificates.

It's taken me many years to successfully analyse what went wrong for me in that qualifying year, but with the help of retired English and Languages teacher Miss Helen Adam in 2022 I finally discovered the explanation. Helen Adam, a good friend, was a remarkable lady. Confined, from the age of seventeen, to a wheelchair due to the debilitations of polio, she defied all the odds and went on to university and teacher training college, and eventually taught English at Carnoustie High School. A greatly admired and much-loved lady, she passed away in February 2023.

I was always in the top six pupils in the "qualie" class of around 30 pupils. Looking back, I recall patiently waiting at the end of the academic year expecting "Hutchie" to one day say, "Well done, Robert Murray! It's time to discuss your attendance at Arbroath High School." However, no such suggestion or

My sister Isobel, front row far right. School ties and uniforms make an appearance.

direction ever came to me. I do recall mum once saying, "If I put one (of her three children) to Arbroath High School, I'll have to put all three of them there, and I just can't afford that." So there was no parental "push," and she made no approach to the school.

When, in my sixties and on holiday in South Africa, I met up with my old school friend Alan Craigie. We chatted and each asked the question: "Why hadn't we attended Arbroath High School?" He told me his mother complained he would never get up in time to get the train at 8.20 am, while I quoted my mother's view about the cost of all three of her children going to High School.

At that point, as Alan and I wrestled with the mystery, I got as far as suggesting perhaps the reason was that most pupils would have to remain at Carnoustie to ensure that all subjects would be supported by qualified teachers in, for example, science, French, history and English. Alas, the reason was far more simple and obvious. Only quite recently, in 2022, did I finally discover the true facts from Helen Adam. I now tell the divisive story, as follows:

"So, Helen, why did I never receive word that I could be offered a place at Arbroath High School?" I asked her. "You went to Carnoustie School too, and you went on to Arbroath High, didn't you?"

"Yes, I did, but I had a struggle to get there," she told me.

"Why was that? You went on to be a teacher!" I was genuinely puzzled.

"Yes, but my mother had to go to Mr Ness the Headmaster and plead with him for me to get to Arbroath High."

"That seems strange."

"Oh, no—many mothers of my friends had to do the same."

"Why was that?"

"Well, you see, Mr Ness's salary depended on the number of pupils he could enrol in his senior school."

"Ah, so he didn't want to lose pupils?" I enquired, the picture becoming clearer.

"Exactly!"

"So, there was no automatic streaming of the best pupils with the highest 11+ rating going on to the High School?"

"That's correct."

My brief conversation with Helen answered the question which had plagued me for years.

Sadly, Alan Craigie passed away in 2010 and would never know any of that revelatory background information.

Amazingly, while chatting recently with one of my old school pals, I discovered another story told to me in 2024. Evidently, "Hutchie" had gone to my friend's home and told his mother that despite his sister having done very well in the qualifying year, he had decided she was not to advance to Arbroath High with no reason given.

There were, of course, social and economic undercurrents at work. Children of wealthier and influential parents in the town were selected for High School regardless of ability—and allegedly, some even paid for their under-performing son or daughter to advance.

It made a mockery of the qualifying system. Alas, it was the penalty for living in the only Angus Burgh with no high school at that time.

My class reunion, which I arranged in 2005.
From the back, L to R: Colin Airth, Gordon Spankie (?), Robbie Murray, John Salmond, Les Vannet, John Blair, John Ferrier, Jim Fairweather, Bill Duncan, Chic Johnstone, Bill Ross, Alan Craigie, Norman Lamb, Art teacher Mr George Robb, Bill McGregor, Julie Braid, Ernie Orrock, Jenny Black, Elizabeth Paul, Moira Wilson, Richard Simmons, [Unknown], Dorothy Shepherd, Margo Gordon.
Front row: Sheila Scott, Margaret Christie, Maths Teacher Mr Currie, Teacher Mrs McDougall, Dorothy Towns, Jean Adamson, May White, Thelma Mintram, Aileen Hood.

I felt even more cheated that I was never allowed to wear the distinctive green school blazer when I saw many of my former school pals walking home along the High Street as I pedalled around on my message bike. Well, I made the most of it, and have had nothing to complain about—but deep down, I think I developed a determination to apply myself in working life as hard as I could... just to prove a point!

On a comforting note, when I recently told my story to a friend in the town about my missed opportunity at Arbroath High, he told me, "I wouldna' worry, Robbie. I hated the High School, and the teachers were horrible!"

Subjects in the years from age 12 up to leaving Carnoustie school at age 15 were: science, English, maths (including geometry, algebra and trigonometry), French (compulsory in first year only), history, geography, technical drawing, and woodwork and metal work. I enjoyed every subject, and somehow found time to take home some prized woodwork items—a

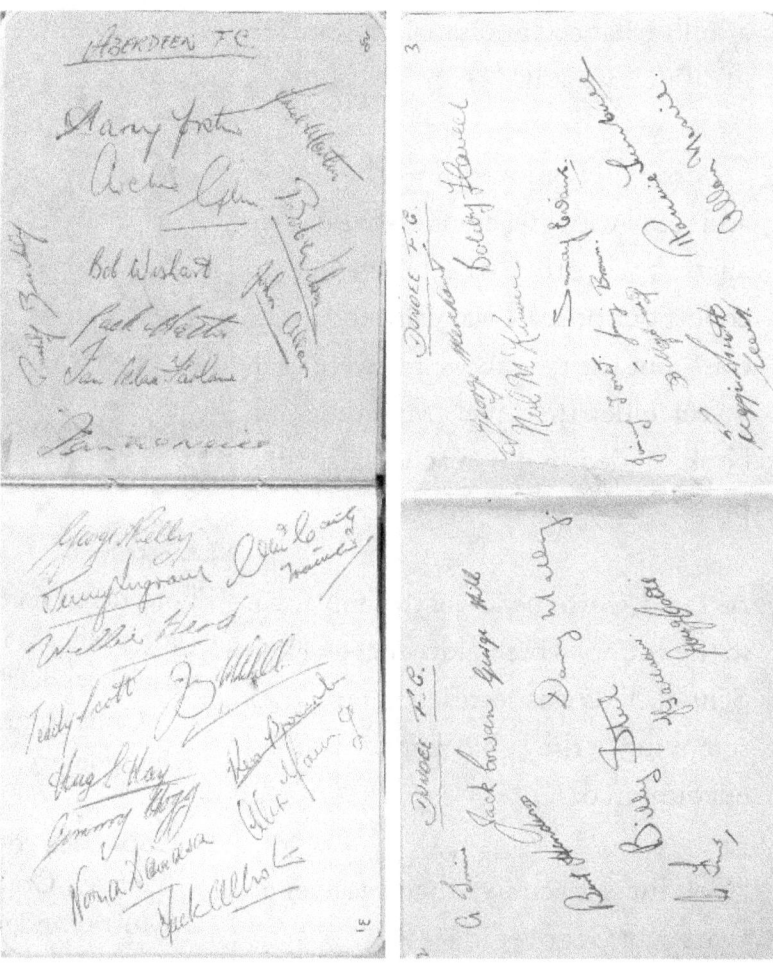

A prized collection of autographs provided by my Physical Education teacher, George Merchant (1954/55): Players from Aberdeen Football Club (left) and Dundee Football Club (right).

table lamp, card table, occasional table, and a lamp standard. In hindsight, I now rationalise that Carnoustie Secondary School provided a well-balanced and satisfying start in life. But... what if?

I thoroughly enjoyed my school days and recall with great sadness the day we all trooped off to the beach hall to collect our prizes. I was third top in the class, but the two above me were each a year older than me! My autograph book, signed by my teachers, is still a prized possession.

As I said, Carnoustie was the only town in the county which didn't have a High School. This was rectified in 1972, thus removing the blockage I had encountered.

"Goodness gracious – that was over 70 years ago! Get over it!"

Photo taken on Scout Grounds with New Taymouth Golf Club premises in the background. Cub Mistress Winnie Laurie (back left), Cub Mistress Betty Miller (back right).
Cubs front row: Mike West, George Gillon, Rob Montgomery, Alan Muir, Ian Muir, Fraser Thornton, 〚Unknown〛.
Cubs back row: Ian Anderson, Harry Buick, Robbie Murray, Graham Smith, Bobby Ross, James (Peem) Murray, Edgar Thomson. Fred Laurie in back row.

Cubs

"Dib Dib Dib Dob—Akala!"

Like so many things in my life, luck played a massive part. You see, my mum had become friends with Mr and Mrs Reid and their family: Harry, Margaret and Angus. Mr Reid worked for his brother Alex, who ran the garage and petrol pump in Dundee Street at No 148. The Reid family sat beside us Murrays in the same upstairs pew at Newton Panbride Church (latterly named Carnoustie Panbride

Church). (Note: as I write this in 2024, "the union" of Barry Church, Carnoustie Parish and Carnoustie Panbride Churches has been announced, resulting in one church—i.e. Carnoustie Trinity Church. This results in the parish churches of Barry and Panbride being closed, with Panbride Church being offered for sale by the Church of Scotland and Barry Church remaining as a social meeting centre for the village. The long-running decline of congregational members across Scotland since the 1950s has finally caught up with the Church of Scotland, which is now being forced to act.) Harry was nine years old and a year older than me. One day, Mrs Reid had invited mum, James (aka Peem), Isobel and me for tea in their first floor flat at Balfour Place, just off Dundee Street. We played games in the house and sometime, after tea around 6 pm, Harry put on his Cub cap and neckerchief and was about to set off to his weekly meeting in the Scout hut.

I had heard of Cubs but had no idea how to find out about them. It was Mrs Reid (probably tempted to reduce the boisterous noise) who said, "Why don't you take Robert and James to see what's going on?" Mum added, "Well now, when it finishes, make your own way home to Westhaven." And that was it—the rest is wonderful history.

Peem and I took to Cubs like ducks to water—or should I say, like cubs to a den. We enjoyed everything—sitting on logs, chanting our "Akalas" and "Bagheeras," dibbing and dobbing, playing Kim's Game, and running around excitedly.

Our Scout kitchen, roped off, with plate rack and mug tree.

At summer camp. Stag Patrol ready for inspection.
From L to R: Robbie Murray (Patrol Leader), Freddie Gall, Mike West, Ian Deuchars.

After early tests, we were awarded our Tenderfoot badge to sew on our cap, followed by other tests which rewarded us a small silver metal star which was stitched alongside the Tenderfoot badge. As "Baby Cubs," that star was our "First Eye" opened, and we went on to gain a "Second Eye." What marvellous, momentous moments—all due to Mrs Reid and Harry. I experienced one, week-long, camp as a Cub; it was to Tannadice, near Finavon, Angus. We travelled on "Tattie Thamson's" (of Victoria Street) lorry, and sat on top of tents and pots and pans ("dixies," to be precise). We slept, six cubs in a "Niger" tent, and Peem and I ended up in different tents.

At the start of that memorable adventure, I remember my father laid my heavy kit bag crossways and inside the frame of his bike, and carried Peem's kit bag over his shoulder to deliver us and our over-weight bags to the scout hut which, in 1949, was located about 100 yards east of the junction of Links Avenue and Taymouth Street. No wonder our kit was heavy—no sleeping bags in those days. We took heavy, bulky blankets, a ground sheet, tin plates, etc. I recall mum and dad, via a newspaper advertisement, buying for each of us an ex-Army WW2 "sleeping bag", with a linen top and a waterproof base. I still recall the rubber smell. We then put a shaped woollen sleeping bag inside, with another blanket on top of that! We must have driven mum and dad crazy. Once the big groundsheet was laid down, we each trooped off to a nearby stack and filled our "palliasses" with straw. (A palliasse was another name for what, in effect, looked like a large cotton duvet cover.) Very comfortable on the first night, but as the week progressed the luxury began to fade when bumps and hollows developed in the straw. On our third night there was a thunderstorm, and water started to seep under the tent groundsheet and eventually—to our dismay— trickle in streamlets on top of it. We were dried out the next day, but were again soaked in the middle of the following night and were led into the nearby scout hut, where we slept on the floor for the next two nights.

Major Neish was a big figure physically, and a big name in Angus scouting—he seemed to run the Tannadice country estate. We were paraded on Sunday morning and, along with other cubs and scouts who were camped in the area, we attended an outdoor church service led by the Major. Looking back, I suspect the enthusiastic and serious Major Neish was probably grooming us in the "army-like" style of Scouting founder Lord Baden-Powell. Perhaps he saw us as potential national servicemen?

Tannadice was where I made a glaring, innocent error. As detailed, I was helping to tidy up in the outdoor kitchen, which was marked out by twine and small wooden pegs. We had a mug tree and plate racks made with the use of small tree branches, and a 'sump-pit' where we chucked in kitchen waste. Winnie Laurie was our leader and I, along one or two others, was told to clean up all the big dixies and large pots. A short time later, she asked where the "stock" for the soup had gone. I then realised to my horror that I had emptied the entire pot of "stock" down a sump. I had wondered why there were bones at the bottom of the pot as I had tipped it! In dismay, Akala screamed loudly, but she understood how the mistake had happened. Silly wee Robbie Murray's name must have been "mud" that night, as the cub leaders discussed and analysed the day's activities and the one big "kitchen disaster". I'll never know what impact that damning dixie moment had on my career towards opening my "second eye". "Silly boy!"

Scouts

"Stag Patrol ready for inspection, sir!"

It was a natural progression for me to advance from "Cubs" to "Scouts". We had patrols (consisting of four or six Scouts) and were, at the start of every meeting, "inspected," Army-style, by our Skipper, Jim Herd. The scout hut in those days was located off Taymouth Street. As you walked down Links Avenue, (aka School Road,) approaching the railway tunnel, you turned left just before the tunnel and after about 100 yards there was, on the left, a large, unused, rough grassy area. From memory it was about 100 yards by 100 yards, and stretched as far back to nearly the back gardens of Kinloch Park houses. The scout hut was situated at the end of a 50-yards-long wide pathway. The remaining grassy area next door to The New Taymouth Golf clubhouse was where we practiced pitching our tents and sorting out camping gear. The hut itself was a long, narrow wooden structure—possibly not much more than 5 or 6 yards wide, and approximately 20 or 30 yards long. It consisted mainly of a central drill area, where we paraded as a group. Each patrol occupied a corner area where it was "inspected" by our Skipper. Beyond that was a toilet and our Scout leader's "den," where Skipper and his assistants—including John

From L to R: Edgar Thomson, Robbie Murray, Archie Douglas, Ian Muir. Ian Anderson, Allan Muir, Mike West and Rob Montgomery.

Fox, Ron Bingham and Fred Buick—kept their paperwork and walking gear. The Rovers had a lockable room at the end nearest Taymouth Street.

Although the hut boasted electric lighting, my one vivid memory is of the coal or wood burning stove which was the sole means of heating. The stove itself was of a cylindrical metal construction (cast iron, I think) about 3 or 4 feet high and 12 inches diameter, consisting of a slot at the bottom where ash could be removed and a lid at the top through which logs or coal could be dropped. Leading from the stove was the chimney—a 6 inch diameter pipe which was attached by a bracket to the inside wall and then led through the roof. Sadly, the stove rarely worked. When it was lit, smoked belched out of it... but unfortunately not through the chimney. There never seemed to be a "draught" to get the smoke "up and out."

There was a plan that some of us, including myself, would pop into the hut after school on Tuesdays during winter to get the fire lit to warm up the building. But invariably our efforts resulted in the freezing hut being full of smoke—probably one good reason why, for fifteen minutes, we played "British Bulldog" (a rugby- type game) for a warm-up. Looking back, I now wonder if it was simply a bird's nest blocking the chimney! A sad story of Scouts that couldna' light a fire.

There were two Scout troops in Carnoustie. 1st troop was the original, and my brother Peem was in that troop. I was in the 2nd troop, which was "raised" in 1952 when the war bulge of 12 years-olds necessitated a second troop. I still have my Scout record card showing dates when I passed various tests. The first stages were basic or preliminary tests, and once we worked our way through that we managed to proceed on to "proficiency" badge tasks such as tracking, woodsman, first aid, cooking, etc. We had an annual camp and, when I think of it today, I am full of praise for our Cub mistresses and Scout leaders who must have given up valuable summer holiday time to administer meetings and then attend and run our camps. I recall annual camps at Glen Clova, Glen Farg and Pitlochry. Clova campsite was situated on the banks of the river South Esk, which provided our washroom and kitchen water. One day,

Skipper (Jim Herd) declared that we were to have a swim in the river. Assistant leader John Fox, a strong tanned figure, was asked by Skipper to swim across the river with a safety-rope tied around his waist, then to tie the end of the rope to the bottom of a large tree and swim back. This he did, but Skipper then wisely decided the swift flowing deep water was not safe to allow us "skinny white shivering Tarzans" to splash about even with a safety rope. From that day onwards I often remarked to John (who was also my Sunday School teacher, and fellow member of Newton Panbride church dramatic club) that I thought his swim was hugely impressive and something out of Hollywood. Over the years I became very friendly with John, who used to reply, "Oh, it was nothing, Robbie. But aye, the water was a wee bit chilly." When he was ninety years old, I repeated my customary compliment. Only then did he confess, "Och, Robbie, it wisnae that deep at all—I had my feet on the bottom!" I could scarely believe it. "Jings, Johnnie!" I replied. "And you've been my local 'Tarzan' hero for all these years!" We had a great laugh about that story, and I had the honour to tell the tale when I delivered the eulogy at his funeral. I always had huge respect for John Fox.

While at camp, we usually cooked as one entire troop—taking turns chopping wood to keep the fire going, cook, wash dishes, etc., but sometimes we did all our cooking on a "patrol" basis, which meant that we had to have the skills within our small groups. That's when food wasn't always of the best quality, but we swiftly learned from our mistakes. Our kitchens were areas marked off by twine and sticks in the ground, with an obvious "door area." We constructed pot racks and plate racks, all put together by branches sitting on "y"-shaped stick uprights. We also had a thing called a "mug tree"—a branch of a tree, trimmed and stuck in the ground with hooks. All this kept our equipment off the ground. Once, at Pitlochry, we caught a rabbit and had a lesson on how to gut, clean and cook it on a 'spit'.

On arrival at our sites the first job, after erecting tents, was to dig "sumps." We had a sump for kitchen waste dug inside our marked off kitchen, and another for the latrines—otherwise referred to as the "lats."

A "lat" had to have a lid. This would often be ferns or big leaves laid on a framework of wooden sticks—the purpose of which was to hopefully keep flies (and more!) away. Of course, if we were camped near bushes or shrubs, we didn't need a screen, but in an open field we used a "lat" tent or screen.

One highlight during a week's camp was "visiting day," when mums bearing Mars Bars, sweeties, or homemade dumpling and cakes, arrived by bus. We had to be on our best behaviour and make them a cup of tea. Another highlight was a walk to the nearest shop—if there was one! Then, we could buy a bottle of lemonade and sweeties, and I always took the opportunity to send a postcard to my grannies and grandads.

Our Scout leaders were also Rover Scouts, or "Rovers." I recall some names: Ron Bingham, Dave Fyffe, Alg Burrows, Jim Ramsay, Fred Buick, Chic Leven, Alastair and Ian McCallum, and Fred Laurie, to name a few. Over time, they had built a much-needed wooden bridge over the River South Esk further up Glen Clova, towards Bachnagairn Forest. The Rovers had a much-prized 1920s

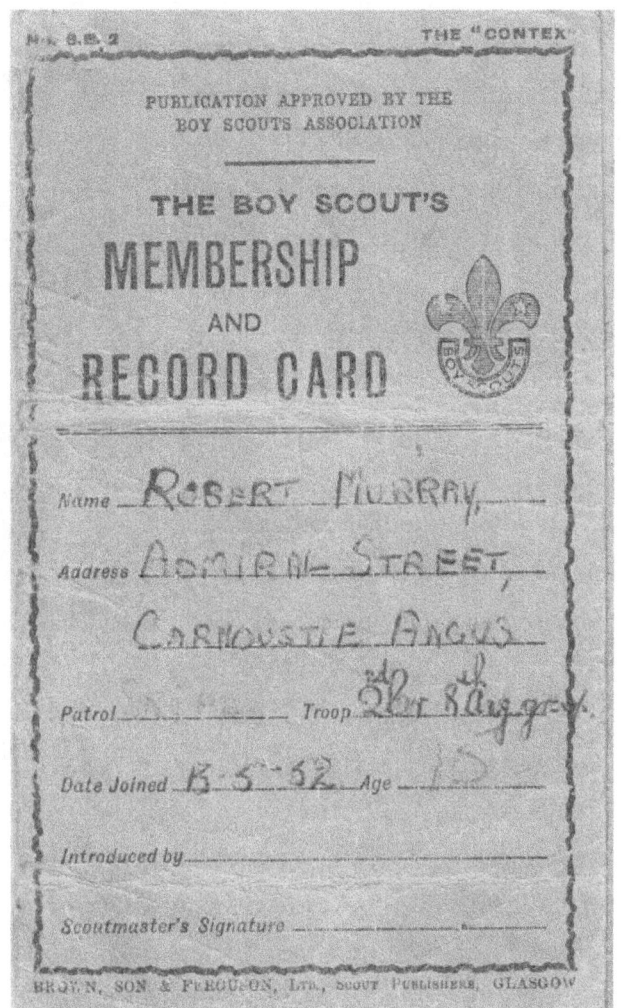

My Boy Scout Record Card, 1952.

open-top car, rather in the style of the "Mary Poppins" car, or "Genevieve." One day, a plan was announced that John Fox would drive part of the way up the glen towards the bridge in order to inspect it for any winter damage.

There was space for two scouts to accompany him, and a quiz was held to decide which two would be chosen—and I was one. What a treat: a run in the Rovers' car, and a two-mile hike up the glen to see the bridge—which, incidentally, was in good condition.

I still retain memories deeply etched in my mind of the evenings when, all gathered around a campfire, a blanket over our shoulders and a mug of cocoa in our hands, we sang scout songs. Favourite ones for me being "Green Grow the Rashes Oh," or "We're Riding Along on the Crest of a Wave." Luckily for us, our leaders had a store of "spooky" stories. As the sun was setting, our Union Jack was lowered and we sang "Taps": "Day is done, gone the sun/From the sea from the hills from the sky/All is well, Safely rest. God is nigh" (to the tune of a trumpet "Last Post"). Another great memory, while at the Pitlochry camp, was the ascent of Ben-y-Vrackie. This was my first big climb,

Photo taken as we leave Scout grounds to trek to Panmure House Grounds for a weekend camp. Kinloch Park houses can be seen in the background.

and set me on a desire to walk the mountains of Scotland whenever I got the chance. In more recent years, 1974, I climbed Ben Vrackie with my then-8-year-old daughter Carys, and later with her two children Lucy (14) and Jonny (10) in 2010.

During all my later life I have often expressed my great appreciation and good fortune of never having to go and fight in a war. My Boy Scout days were the nearest I and my friends got to experience some kind of discipline, and it all started with that casual visit to Cubs with Harry Reid.

"I cannot possibly imagine my life with no Scouting experiences!"

Air Training Corps (ATC)

"I'm no joinin' the Air Force—the beans are terrible!"

Much as I enjoyed Scouting life, my interest gradually began to diminish. Partly because our leaders took on family duties, and also due to the fact that we as scouts became employees and couldn't get holiday dates to fit in with camps. Most of all, because our troop was raised as an extra one in the town (due to the war bulge), which meant we all left school and started work within a year or so around 1955. With our thoughts, at the time, on National Service (when we expected to be "called up" for two years military service), Peem, my brother, and I joined the ATC (Air Training Corps). A squadron existed in Monifieth, and we joined up. We did drill and studied plane spotting, mapping, and compass work. It required only one evening each week, and we were kitted out in full RAF-type uniform.

We enjoyed a trip to RAF Leuchars and a ten-minute flight in a six-seater Anson. (In recent years, I visited Montrose Air Station and was amazed to see how small and fragile an Anson looked.) Sickbags were issued, but happily not required. I recall we all received a plate of beans on toast—AFTER the flight. It's strange how impressions can be formed, for although we each had ideas of which branch of the military we would choose (if given the chance), the poor quality of the thin runny beans immediately put us off the RAF! We were a young generation of (then) relatively privileged kids.

There must have been around 150 of us from various Squadrons that day, and we were all herded into a hangar and addressed by a senior officer followed by a short church service and prayer. I guess we were given a taste of what to expect in National Service. What stays in my mind to this day is the fact that before that religious part of the address began, there came the announcement: "Would any cadets who are not of the Presbyterian faith please move into the hangar next door." I never did find out what happened "next door."

Peem, the following year, attended a week-long stay at RAF Hawarden in North Wales, where he enjoyed more flights and more "watery" beans—which, I'm led to believe, had a few uttering, "I'm definitely going to join the Army."

"Luckily I was never 'called-up' to assess the Army's beans.

Doctors

"Get me a spoon, please, Mrs Murray, so that I may check their tonsils!"

My brother James (Peem) in ATC uniform.

My earliest memory of a Carnoustie doctor was when "the Old" Dr George McConnell called to our home at Annfield Cottage, Barry Road, sometime in 1944–45. He had called to inspect me and my brother shortly after we had been discharged from Dundee Royal Infirmary, having had our tonsils removed. I recall him asking mum to provide a spoon to help him keep our tongue out of the way. In those days, doctors called to visit patients, having had a phone call or personal visit to "make an appointment" by a parent or friend seeking help. In the case of his checking our throats, I can only imagine he was asked to follow up our progress by a hospital doctor.

Dr McConnell was a highly-respected gentleman in the town and, following his death at the age of 39, a well laid-out rose garden financed by citizens was established in his memory. The garden is still (in 2025) looked after by the council, although the young people who frequent it sometimes leave litter lying in and around it, having no idea of what the garden means and why it is there.

The young Dr Desmond McConnell, carrying a large black bag, was always very well turned out in a striped three-piece suit, and was surrounded by the unforgettable but not unpleasant blended aroma of cigarette smoke and Dettol. Luckily, as a family we didn't require many visits, but I recall old Dr McConnell's son Desmond making a house call to check on me. I had a high temperature of around 102 caused, I learned, by liver fluke. This followed a weekend of camping when I and other Scout patrol leaders—Eggie Thomson, Ian Muir, Billy Montgomery and Archie Douglas—had pushed and pulled the scout trek-cart loaded with our tent, pots, clothing etc. from the scout hut in Taymouth Street to a field in Panmure House estate. We had carefully cooked our food, but I had stupidly supped some water from a lively stream and consequently suffered a high temperature by consuming liver fluke from sheep's droppings. I was ill for only two days, and my "toilet stools" were chalky white, indicating a serious infection in my bowels. A life-long lesson for me.

I recall seeing Dr Desmond's Sunbeam Talbot sports car parked outside the surgery, complete with Monte Carlo road race badges and adorned by the small chrome rod and red ball indicating it was a doctor's car. He was, evidently, a keen motor rally participant. Gradually doctors' visits to homes were diminished, and now—in 2025—the procedure for medical attention is to phone the Health Centre at Barry Road at 8 am precisely on weekdays for a returned telephone consultation call from a doctor and then, if necessary, to obtain an appointment time or prescribed medication. Emergencies are dealt by ambulance crews: "first responders".

In the 1950s, there were two medical practices: Dr McConnell's in a villa at the east end of the terrace including Erdington Villa on Dundee Street, and Dr P.D.C. McKay in the substantial villa at the top of Bonella Street.

"The days of routinely securing a home visit by a doctor are long gone!"

Unspoken Happiness: Getting My Tonsils Out

"Come on now, Robert—just give 'Mickey Mouse' a wee cuddle!"

"You've been screaming to each other nearly all night and all day, but if you stop, I'll bring him near you," said the nurse, trying to calm me. I went quiet for some time, then heard a loud, long, sobbing wailing from the other end of the ward. I knew it was my brother. We were both in hospital.

He was there, somewhere. I could hear him howl my name. I lay patiently waiting, but still there was no sign of him. Then I heard him agonisingly screech my name again. I screamed in reply, then I heard my young brother shout my name, but now he sounded in pain and in tears. I wanted to run to him to see how he was—what was going on? But I had rails around my bed.

Time passed—I had no idea how long—and then I remember being wheeled, while in my bed, to another part of the hospital. Where was I now? And why? More to the point, where was my wee brother? A nurse said, "Here you are—here's Mickey Mouse." (In reality, it was a disguised chloroform mask.) "Now hold him up to your face and give him a cuddle," the nurse told me. I didn't ask why; I just did as I was told. I drifted in to sleep.

When I woke up, I could tell by the ceiling lights I was in a ward again. But which one? I was very sleepy. I had no idea how long I had lain there. I seemed to sleep, but kept opening my eyes. Then, in a moment of alertness, I glanced at the bed next me... and there he was—my wee brother! How did he get here, and how did I get near him? Where had he been, and when had we been moved?

I wanted to ask where my mum was. I opened my mouth and tried to speak but, somehow, I couldn't say anything. "There you are now," said the same nurse who had earlier denied me being close to my wee brother. "You can speak to him now." I opened my mouth and tried to say, "Wake up, Peem!" But for some reason I couldn't make a noise. Then my brother opened his eyes. I could see he was trying to say something to me. We were both stuck in an unspoken silence. "You've had your tonsils out now, boys, and your mum will be here for you soon. Remember: she said you would get ice cream when you get home!"

"Can I take Mickey Mouse home?" I asked her hopefully.

"Oh no; Mickey stays here," she explained. "He helps all the boys and girls go to sleep."

I remember a comforting silence descend, and I drifted off while dreaming of a large ice cream cone.

Our tonsils were removed at Dundee Royal Infirmary circa 1944/45.

Getting a Haircut

"Just the usual – short back and sides?"

I can't remember going to a barber before I was about nine or ten years old. You see, mum had a small white gloss painted medicine cabinet with a glass mirror door. It contained Elastoplast, crepe and cotton bandages, pink and white lint, safety pins, and her "cure-all" ointment, Valderma. Inside this box of essentials were dad's hair trimming items. When it was time for Peem and me to have a haircut, an old bedsheet was placed around our shoulders and another on the floor to catch clippings. To prevent dad's back pains, we sat on a small stool which was propped up on a dining chair. Dad's hand-clippers were of the type where he squeezed the two grips together, thus moving the cutting blades. This did the job around the neck and ears. A comb and a pair of scissors did the rest. Yes, there were some itchy hairs down my back—but it was free!

Somewhere around 1949 or 1950, Jimmy Tait began to appear fortnightly, towing a caravan which he set up on the piece of waste ground on the seaside of the railway line, near the two old cottages at the foot of the slope at the Steenie Brig, Westhaven. (The Crawfords, Chic and family, lived in the cottage nearest the railway.) My belief is that Jimmy originated in Halifax, and had met his future wife Rita while he was stationed at Barry Buddon Army camp during World War 2. I think a haircut would have cost about sixpence in old money (or 2.5 pence in 2025), but it was worth it as it was an adventure just to step inside Mr Tait's caravan. Dad, of course, was relieved of his chore, but I still got some hairs inside my shirt!

Later, probably when I was 12 or 13 years old, Jimmy opened a shop across the road from The Stag's Head pub in Dundee Street. The entire building was run as one business. Mrs Tait ran a wool and knitting shop in part of the building, and Jimmy had a separate, spacious salon. By the time I was 13, I was keen to get a look at risque Reveille newspapers which were usually laid out randomly and easily available on a small low table in the salon. Between glancing at any images or front-page pictures (which my mum would have severely reprimanded me for gazing at, had she known), I eagerly watched to see if the grown-up man having his hair rubbed with Jimmy's routine splash of Bay Rum, and in the final stage of his short back and sides, was going to make a surreptitious purchase of contraceptives. It was merely a piece of drama I liked to expect at my inquisitive age. The "sales" question from Jimmy was an almost loud whisper ("Something for the weekend, sir?"). A long queue of men meant that all the Reveilles were being read. I would get a bad look from a man if I, as a "nipper", picked up the last available Reveille before he did.

Ritchie Harper—another barber in the town— was a cheery, dapper chap, and always spoke nicely to me when I met him casually in the street. Living in a small town, I occasionally—when older—felt obliged to give him my business. Ritchie's salon was the long, narrow, small shop built on the south side of the High Street, and on the west bank of Lochty Burn, now marked as number 5 High Street. Ritchie became a Carnoustie Town Councillor.

Both barbers were efficient and ran clean and tidy establishments. In those days there were no posters stuck on the walls describing various gent's styles—those were Brylcreem days, and "short back and sides" was the standard reply to "How would you like it?" or "Just a tidy up, then?"

In the 1960s, young Ian McDougall—after a spell running a barber shop in Monifieth—started up his hairdressing business in Park Avenue, Carnoustie, in what is (in 2025) now the Fobel Shop, and many years previously Astbury's photo studio. Ian progressed extremely well and, along with his wife Mary, later ran a newsagent shop and barber shop under one roof at No 100 High Street. He sold the business, and the new owner moved "McDougall's" in 2022 to No 96 High Street, the former Wm Low supermarket (which later became the TSB Bank offices).

Years earlier, when I had worked in Dundee, I encountered Ian by chance when I popped into a barber's shop in Panmure Street in the city. Ian was only 15 years old, and had started there to serve his apprenticeship. "So, this is where you are!" I said teasingly. "You're here to train yourself on guinea pigs in Dundee?" He enjoyed the joke. In attempting to attract custom when he opened his first premises in Monifieth he had asked me how to decorate his window. He didn't have a physical product to sell, and all I remember advising him was to put something original and eye-catching on display like a vintage push-bike or set of golf clubs, or something that seemed "off-beat". In addition to running his newsagent shop in Carnoustie, Ian opened every morning to receive newspapers. He hung up his scissors in 2019 after over 50 years of cutting hair and rising at 4 am to deal with newspapers and morning rolls.

It was only when I returned to Carnoustie to help my brother Peem look after our mum that I began my regular haircuts by Ian. We had an on-going joke—especially if there were one or two customers seated and waiting. I didn't need a haircut, but would enter his salon and say, "Excuse me, barber; I'm new here. Can you help me, please? It's this bald top; do you know of a barber in the town who could do something about that?"

Ian's rehearsed reply was: "Well, I'm not sure, but I could draw a rabbit on that bald patch."

"Oh, a rabbit," I would say. "How would that help?"

"Well, from a distance it might look like a hare!"

"Oh yes, well, then I'll be in later. Thank you, barber."

Ian kept a serious face and I played the idiot part, and it was always good fun to watch the newspapers being lowered to reveal the gaping faces of the men in the queue. (Perhaps the man in the chair was in a hurry and didn't think it at all funny.)

I tried a new Turkish barber (in 2022)—a very good one too. Sadly, during his second year in business, he had to close his shop due to the 2020 COVID-19 pandemic. I have now settled on Guys and Cutz at number 68 High Street. The ladies there are very good, and they splash on the Bay Rum—just like Jimmy Tate did all those years earlier!

As I think of my Carnoustie barbers, they each reflect important parts of history in my lifetime—firstly, Jimmy, just back from the Second World War, then Ian who reflected the energy and opportunities in the 1960s for young people to open in business, and then the Turkish barber—an immigrant to this country, searching for safety and prosperity in the UK.

I've always believed it's important to know your barber.

Bikes and Baths

"Dinna jump in Peem—the blanket's no up yet!"

In the 1950s, the most popular, and in fact the most essential and only mode of transport (apart from Shank's Pony!) was the bicycle. Peem, Isobel and me all had, at some time, a "trike"—a three-wheeled pedal bike which, as we grew up, was "handed down." When we moved to Westhaven it must have become clear to mum and dad that the most efficient way to get to and from shops or school to home was to have a bike. It was essential to travel to school, to Scouts or to shops, and to meet pals somewhere in the town.

Living at Anchor Place had one big advantage, and that was the large wash house which was shared by each of the four households in the block. Mum's allocated day for washing and use of the clothes poles was Tuesday every week. The wash house probably measured about 10 feet by 10 feet.

Located at the small window, which faced towards the back of the tenement, was a wash tub where mum washed out "smalls," and attached to the sink was the "wringer"—a two-roller device which squeezed out the water from soaked sheets, clothing, etc. In the far corner was a large three-sided concrete block into which was fitted a large circular, two-feet deep washtub. Underneath the tub was a fireplace, into which she placed firewood or coal as fuel. Everything had to be handled by her; using a bucket, she had to fill the big washtub with water from the tap at the sink—and many buckets of water were required to fill that tub. I still recall the warm soapy smell of the suds bubbling in the big tub. The sheets and pillowcases then had to be rinsed in cold water in the bath or the washtub. Once rinsed, mum then hung out the clothes to dry using her own line, which she strung out between the clothes poles provided on the drying green. She had the use of communal stretchers, which were used to prop up the clothes lines.

Young Robbie models the Murray family "trike".

The other use of the washhouse was as a bath house. Usually, on any Saturday evening, mum would stoke up the fire and heat the water in the large wash tub. She would then, bucket by bucket, begin to generously fill a well-proportioned bath. Of course, with the use of a blanket, she then "rigged up" a temporary curtain at the window. This was the usual routine, and it was a fabulously warm and cosy experience—sheer luxury, in fact. I can't remember exactly how often (or seldom) we enjoyed those bathhouse scrubs; we did not have the luxury of a regular evening plunge.

Bath nights were possible only because all the bicycles, probably seven or eight, used by the occupants living in the block were removed (only on a dry evening) from the wash house. The crucial thing was that the bicycles had to be re-packed in an exact order so that the user who was first 'out' in the morning had their bike nearest the door. The system wasn't perfect, but for mum it must have been a huge step forward compared to what she had endured at our cottage at Barry Road. In fact, when I think of it, in her lifetime mum had experienced the drudgery of old-fashioned laundry and bath night routines to then enjoying, in her later years, the luxuries of a washing machine and a bathroom. I have a suspicion that our Anchor Place bathtub in the washhouse was her first experience of such a luxury.

"Mum made that extra effort in everything she did. Bath night was one!"

Saturday Duties

"Bike gently and dinna' damage the cakes, Robert!"

With dad working morning shifts on alternate weeks and mum working at Mrs Aimer's B&B in Philip Street, I was, before the age of 12, left with a string of Saturday duties.

These began with brushing then wiping the linoleum in the living room, washing dishes, and, when required, clearing out ashes then setting the coal fire ready to be lit. Once the household chores were completed, I had routine shopping duties. First, to the Co-op Central grocery shop for groceries. The most exciting part of that job was to stand mesmerised as the money was put in a container, and then into a tube which whizzed around the shop to a lady in a centrally-located raised office. Back, in a few minutes, would come change and a Co-op ticket. The amount spent would be logged in the central records, and mum would keep her ration book up to date with coupons. Later she, like all shoppers, would receive the "Co-op Dividend" (or "divvy") which was an annual amount paid back (like a discount), and which was calculated every year by being "so much in the £1 spent." If, for example, the "Divvy" was declared at say "6d in the £1," mum would receive a 6d (2.5p) for every pound she spent in the Co-op. In those days, Co-ops were operated in towns and cities all over the country, and each Co-op was described as an Association which was run by a local management committee.

With grocery shopping dealt with, it was then time for me to buy the precious box of freshly-baked cakes. The usual shop I had to visit was Nicoll's at the Cross on the west corner of Queen Street and High Street and across the road (in those days) from de Marco's, the posh ice cream parlour (then later a Spar supermarket and now, in 2025, a Premier Convenience store). The queue at Nicoll's was always long—that is, the length of a very long counter (30 feet?), and doubled back inside the shop to the outside door and into the street. With probably 20 customers in front of me, it was a long wait, and while we enjoyed Nicoll's cakes hugely mum often said, if the queue was too long, I should cycle along to Findlay's baker shop near the West End Co-op. Today it is a barber's shop. I was given the responsibility to choose the family's six cakes. The usual choice was cakes, but sometimes mum would ask me to get 6 cream cookies instead. Wherever I bought the cakes, or cookies, my trickiest moment was to safely cycle home with the special white cardboard box tied with a raffia type ribbon and six items intact. With five in the family, there was always one cake or cookie left in the box. Who would get it? Dad, usually—to take to work with his "piece"!

My perk for doing the shopping was that I was always able to make sure my favourite cake found its way into the box—almost always a strawberry tart. We, as a family, may not have had much money, but I'm certain our week-end treats of mum's steak pies, trifles, and the town's best cakes made us feel privileged.

"I'm sure those simple duties built in me a sense of responsibility!"

The Murray family enjoy a caravan holiday in Dunkeld.

CHAPTER 2
High Days and Holidays

Easter

"We're going to roll our Easter eggs at the Fairy Steps again!"

After the dark, cold days of winter, complete with snow and ice, March or April were welcome months—providing revived thoughts of getting out and about in the countryside, and new sandals for Sundays. It is all too familiar: Spring in Scotland can produce wildly contrasting weather, from warm, sunny periods interspersed with bitterly cold, cloudless nights and freezing winds. Easter dates do fluctuate from year to year. Nevertheless, that allows opportunities to enjoy the ritual of a picnic when we roll our Easter eggs.

Over the years I enjoyed a variety of such picnics. They included the time when, on a bitterly cold and wet Sunday in Camperdown Park, Dundee, isolated family members (arranged by my mother) had gathered from near and far. We should have been enjoying outdoor fun together, devouring our picnic egg and treats, but instead found ourselves in the relative comfort of our own cars with the heater turned full on. Rather similar, many years later, when in my cottage in Carnoustie on an Easter day of fierce wind and rain I rolled my egg down a makeshift wooden "hill" covered in green baize. But happily, in addition to those exceptionally grim Easter weather experiences, I have found Easter fun on many memorable occasions in my early life.

My earliest egg-rolling moments were when mum cautiously took us off to the "ballaster" at Westhaven to enjoy a "wee roll" down a miniature hill. The disappointing speed of a "slow" egg was favourably balanced with the instant availability of the swings and the nearby beach and rock pools.

For several years, the favourite Easter picnic venue for my family was the "fairy steps". These are approached by a walk which starts at the "loupin stane", beside the cottages at the entry to Panbride Parish Church, followed by a descent via the "fairy steps" to the wicket gate at the entrance to the wooden bridge which spans Monikie (Craigmill)Burn. Once over the bridge, we enjoyed a sheltered spot with an ideal "Easter egg slope" which provided much fun with competing races until our shells (and the patience of the mums) disintegrated. The excitement of those treks was increased by the fact there were usually several mums with their children, all making their way in a long slow-moving expedition to the renowned spot situated beside the ancient footpath. Only in recent times have I found that the path to the steps, and the steps themselves, were part of a well-trodden path in ancient times from Panmure Estate and the Muirdrum to the seaside, and in later times to the Bleachfield works. There is a theory that a Mr Fairweather created the steps to avoid the slippery mud path—hence in time they were labelled Fairy's Steps. Sorry to dispel with the notion of supernatural "fairies."

Easter at my gran and grandad's Woodside Croft, at Dunninald also provides clear memories. The thrill of the bus journey to get there was the opening chapter of the big day. We disembarked at the White Inn, the white cottage at the top of the Arbroath/Montrose road at the spot where a road leads to Boddin. As the years rolled on, my brother and sister and I became more familiar with the one mile walk to the croft, and I recall many occasions of scampering on ahead of mum, unwittingly showing our confidence to meet up with our locally-based cousins. Granny didn't have any rolling grassy slopes, but we enjoyed a beautifully secluded Victorian lawn just outside the front door of her quaint croft cottage. I use the term "Victorian," as it was not a pristine, highly-manicured lawn but one cut only occasionally by an old-fashioned push-mower, thus allowing oft repeated carpets of daisies, buttercups and vetches. But the highlight of such days was not the lawn—it was granny's appearance, clutching a large wicker basket bearing a pyramid of eggs in a variety of colours.

Looking back, I now realise Granny must have, over the years, hosted successive grandchildren (my much older cousins) at Easter, and most likely she herself as a child must have enjoyed Easter picnics in her native part of the world at Tigerton, near Little Brechin. Prior to the days of felt-tip pens, granny's method of colouring her eggs was to use natural dyes. I vaguely recall my mother telling me that granny used beetroot, bottled raspberries, and natural cooking dyes to decorate her Easter eggs. The sight of granny holding that basket of subtly coloured eggs on an Easter day lives with me still.

I considered us to be privileged children. We enjoyed simplicity. The treat of a boiled egg coloured, or not, to roll down a hill and a picnic to an unusual setting was an adventure. We even knew the Biblical meaning of what we were replicating.

To be given a chocolate Easter egg of any size off a supermarket shelf would have been for us quite welcome, but we would rather have been inspired by an Easter walk, a picnic, and a real, specially prepared, hen's egg.

"Roll on , roll on—time for an Easter picnic!"

Christmas

"I'm away to the ballaster to play with my new clubs!"

Over all my years, from the mid-1940s to the present day (2025), I am luckily able to report on the changing characteristics of the many Christmases I have experienced. My earliest memories are those of my Barry Road days—i.e. 1944 until 1947. Somewhere vaguely in my early memory is my dad freshening up our living room walls prior to Christmas, but to be honest I can't pin down an exact year. Today, similar preparations are made to homes with a fresh coat of paint or perhaps new wallpaper or a new carpet, but back then—for reasons either of cost or war-time unavailability, or both—my father resorted to "stippling." What does that mean?

For a base, he white-washed the walls. Then, using stencil shapes, he dabbed on coloured paint and created his own designs. It must have been a painstaking task to cover all the walls in the living room. My guess is that mum had likely suggested something about "brightening up the place for Christmas."

In addition to dad's "stippling" was the arrival of a small Christmas tree which was placed at the cottage window. My recollection was of a tiny tree, probably only two or three foot tall, which—if memory serves me correctly—was sourced somewhere on Buddon Links. (Shush!) The sharp pine scent is still vividly with me even now. To add to the decorations, I recall going for a family walk when dad snipped off tips of gorse bushes, which we took home and spent happy hours rolling Plasticine into small, different coloured balls which we then stuck onto the spikes of the gorse twig. We were so proud of our little miniature Christmas trees. We may not have had much money and "big" gifts, but our Christmases were full of creative activity, preparation, and huge anticipation.

When as a family we moved to 4 Anchor Place, Admiral Street, we enjoyed more and larger rooms. We could now put up a bigger tree. I have little memory of Christmas paper decorations in our Barry Road house, but I do vividly recall our elaborate efforts at Westhaven. A flat paper bell shape opened out into a three-dimension multi-coloured bell which was pinned into the ceiling at the exact centre of the living room. From each of the four high corners of the room, our most elaborate and colourful decorations were hung equally to meet in the centre of the ceiling beside the bell. Along the top of each wall were our home-made chain decorations, which were equally looped around the walls.

We were of an age at Admiral Street to sit down each year and write our letters to Santa, which we popped carefully up the chimney while our coal fire, lit especially in the big bedroom, was glowing. Happy carefree days. Wondering if Santa would bring the items on the list didn't make sleep easy on Christmas Eve, and that moment in the shadowy faint light in the morning stirred the first flashes of excitement. The empty sock fastened by an elastic garter over the end of the bed was visible, but its shape looked odd. What could be in there? And what about items not in the sock—where are they? Are there any at all? Sock contents usually included chocolate, toffee, an apple and orange, and probably some little unusual item. The thrill was so great that I was in two minds: to rush in and find the answer, or wait until there were other noises in the house before breaking the morning silence.

Meccano sets had arrived in earlier years along with my John Bull printing kit but most of all I remember the year Santa brought me golf clubs. I was probably 11 or 12 years old, but the thrill of seeing the shapes of four golf clubs in a golf bag silhouetted in the grey gloom meant I could no longer wait. Sure enough—just as requested, a driver, a mashie-niblick and chipper and a putter, plus balls and tees! Despite the hard frost, I dressed and tip-toed out of the house and was, in an instant, driving a ball from the nearest piece of grass at the bottom of Admiral Street— then spent a long time trying to find the wayward balls in the white frosty grass. But the joy!

Santa didn't bring large expensive gifts to 4 Anchor Place, but with golf clubs, books, socks and gloves, an apple and orange, and some chocolate bars I felt quite happy— topped only by the time Santa brought me my first wrist watch, an oblong-faced Oris, which I wore proudly whenever I attended church but never on any other occasion. In adult life, I have learned that some people, in earlier generations, were "lucky" to receive an apple and an orange, but more probably a small lump of coal and a piece of home-made toffee in their stocking. Such tales confirmed my feeling of being well cared for by Santa.

One of my most memorable Christmas experiences was the time we all, as a family, were invited to granny and grandad's Woodside Croft cottage, where my brother and sister—and several cousins from the Montrose area—sat around Granny's large table and enjoyed some amazing food treats, then moved through to find the big bedroom had been warmed by a glorious log fire. Grandad had set up the Christmas tree, which was lit up by "real flame" candles fastened to the branches. Everyone had to "do" a party piece. I usually tried to sing "Down in the Glen"—though some onlookers probably wished I was far away in a glen!

These days there are no longer paper bells and paper chains, or paper decorations draped all over the room, nor real candles or sprigs of gorse. Real "pine scented" freshly-cut Christmas trees can still be found, but mainly artificial trees are preferred which are packed away in a cupboard and used yearly.

It's the small details that stay in my mind—like dad's strung-out cardboard cut-out lettering declaring "Merry Christmas," with each letter in a different painted colour. This sign he removed from its place on the living room wall on New Year morning to be replaced by "Happy New Year" in a similar style. It's those small but valued moments which remain most deeply etched in my memories of happy family Christmas times.

"Santa looked after us very well—Ho! Ho! Ho!"

New Year

"That'll teach you a lesson!"

My first active New Year experience was in 1957. My friend John Blair (a message boy with Landsburgh's—a high-class grocer and wines and spirits merchant in Carnoustie) and I decided, against the wishes of my mum and dad, to meet up with a few friends at The Cross in Carnoustie at midnight. We visited a few mutual friends in their houses, but our visitations didn't last very long. This had something to do with my bottle. I should explain.

I was told it was the custom to open my bottle at midnight and share "a dram" with whoever was standing next to me, and likewise accept a dram from a neighbour. That sounds simple enough, although my mother would have been extremely angry about the practice. That friendly and daring custom was innocent enough, but my Achilles' heel was my bottle. I had debated long and hard with John about what was the best drink to buy. Knowing my parents' disapproval, I wanted to buy a bottle (from the shop where John worked), but not strong liquor. Beer, wine, or whisky never featured in discussions, and any "strong" drink I thought should be avoided. In my 17-year-old ignorance, I thought a "cocktail" seemed innocuous enough—not too strong, and it sounded like a "lassie's drink". Of course, in my attempts to be cleverly "grown-up," I was wildly wrong.

Looking back, my parents undoubtedly knew it was wrong to allow me out at New Year, but probably thought "he will learn a lesson." Today, in 2025, the shopkeeper would be (justly) fined for selling alcohol to an under-18-year-old. Trouble was in store for me on my arrival home at around 2 am, and—with great anger—my parents ordered me to bed.

All of this was a stain on my "young life" reputation from a good home, but two sound lessons were learned by me: one was that I never did such a silly thing again, and secondly—by my stupid teenager insistence—I missed my long-awaited New Years' Day football clash between Junior football teams Carnoustie Panmure and Lochee Harp at Westfield Park, Carnoustie—a forerunner to Laing Park. The overriding lesson was, if you plan to do something, make sure you stick to the plan.

With that episode thankfully behind me, I went on to experience another New Year celebration at The Cross. I was now 18 years old and better prepared. No silly bottle in my pocket this time, and with a few friends we gathered at the bottom of Queen Street at 11.45 pm. There must have been around 200 people all standing around in the immediate area. We had no clock chiming or bells ringing in Carnoustie to announce the midnight moment, but a well-known local piper, Rita McBeth, signalled the New Year by bursting into a rendition of "Scotland the Brave". A great cheer went up, and everybody was shaking hands with someone (anyone?) and exchanging, pieces of coal, shortbread biscuits, or dressed herring. (This was, I believe, a token of wishing someone "good harvests ahead" within fishing communities. A cooked herring was "dressed" with a hat and clothing fashioned from tissue paper. Probably never devoured, but most likely tipped in the rubbish bin!) With the initial hand-shaking stage over, it was time to set off on our planned route—agreed by me and my friends. First stop was South America—no, not a sail across the Atlantic, but to a cottage on the golf course. Moving on from that first stop, we set off to visit a cottage somewhere in an isolated area near Barry village. It was time then to return to Carnoustie and first foot some friends in the town. Unlike travel on the links and in the countryside around Barry, we met fellow revellers all over the town and had some good fun and merry exchanges—especially if we knew (or got to know) our fellow "first footers." Luckily, on a dry night we were then able to make our way to the Muirdrum for the final planned visit. By this time we must have been feeling the pace, and I recall in the house of "a friend of a friend" everyone in our group seemed tired at the prospect of a long walk back to Carnoustie and decided to find a space on the floor of the "unknown host" where we boys and girls innocently lay down and slept. (All entirely innocent! Honest!) Refreshed by an hour or two of sleep, it was time to trek home, and I recall at about 8 am we reached the top of Carlogie Road and saw some faint morning light of the New Year creeping in over the North Sea horizon.

It was simply all about not only visiting my own friends but those of my former classmates and workmates. Receiving a dram in every home we visited took its toll, but we were out and about walking around and kept reasonably fit. We were warmly welcomed everywhere we went, and unforgettable were the mountains of delicious and varied New Year food. Perhaps the most damaging impact on us was the frequent moves from the outdoors cold into roasting warm houses with blazing fires. It was so easy to see how weeks of housewives' planning, cooking, baking, and cleaning had all fallen into place.

In contrast to my boisterous wanderings, my mum and dad had a very quiet time—usually wishing their next-door Westhaven neighbours (the Bethels and the Mclagans) a Happy New Year. My mother didn't ever drink alcohol, and my lasting memory of my father's new year tipple was a small quarter bottle of "White Horse" whisky, which he kept in mum's medicine cabinet and was used most sparingly.

"And here's a hand, my trusty friend...!"

Tattie Holidays

"It's ower weet for pickin' the day!" the grieve exclaimed.

There was an arrangement between the Scottish Education Department and the Farmers' Union or Horticultural Association that schools could close for two weeks for potato picking in designated agricultural areas in Scotland. Angus was one such region. During all my years at school, two weeks in October was a holiday nicknamed the "Tattie Holidays." My recollection is that my last weekly tattie holiday pay in 1954 was 13/6 (67.5 pence). For all "Tattie Howkers" (pickers), this was a hugely important wage, as it helped provide mums with extra cash to purchase new shoes and winter clothing for the family.

Although my brother Peem and I picked potatoes at Nether Dysart farm (near our granny's cottage at Dunninald, by Montrose), most of my tattie picking was done at Geordie McGill's Westhaven farm. A typical start to the day was to climb aboard a trailer which was parked overnight under cover of a shed in the farmyard. We had to be in the yard before 7.30 am, and I recall the trailer (bogey)— already filled with pickers—was hooked up to a reversing tractor to make a connection. No health and safety regulations back then, but I don't remember any accidents in this tricky manoeuvre. We were then conveyed, with exhaust fumes swirling around us, to whichever tattie field was being harvested that day. By mid-October the mornings were beginning to be quite chilly, but we soon warmed up after picking began.

To understand how the picking system worked, you must first imagine a tattie field. The "squad" of pickers—let's imagine, say, 40 of them—was divided in two groups. One group of 20 was spaced along the side of the field, while the second group of 20 was spaced in parallel, 20 tattie-drills ("dreels") away. Before any picking began, the "end-rigs" were dug up by the digger. This was to allow diggers and bogeys space to turn. The grieve (farm manager), Mr Milne, then divided the length of the field into 20 equal "bits." Occasionally, if families took juniors along, the "bit" would be half the length. The grieve measured the length out by strides (he probably did some prior arithmetic homework?) and used a whin stick or a branch to mark equal lengths of the "bits". The tattie digger would dig the drill of tatties at the edge of the field, then move to the starting point for pickers 20 drills away and dig there. Once the digger passed, it was time to pick the tatties in your "bit" and fill baskets, or "sculls," as fast as possible.

It became interesting (and probably tiring for the manager) if the field widened or narrowed, as he had to recalculate, evenly, the length of each bit. As you can imagine, the distance between the lines of pickers got closer as the drills were dug up. When there were perhaps only, say, six or eight drills between the lines, the farmer would get one line to move across the field by another 20 or 30 drills away, and so the process continued. No-one was ever left doing nothing. To this day, I marvel the stamina of the full-time farm workers, for once the baskets were filled a horse and cart, or a tractor and bogey, would come around to collect the tatties, and those extra-fit farm workers—without breaking their stride—lifted the baskets by one hand and heave them with seemingly effortless movement into the moving cart or bogey alongside them.

We were given a ten-minute break in the forenoon and afternoon, when we enjoyed hot tea from a flask and a sandwich and biscuit. To this day I can still recollect the unique flavour of the smell of "tattie field tea": it had a distinctive aroma because, to save time, the milk and sugar had already been added. The contrasting odour of the sweet tea and the strong smell of the earth and tattie shaws seemed to be even more heightened. A one-hour lunch break allowed time to get home, wash hands, and enjoy a bowl of soup. The entire experience lives with me to this day: the frosty cold, dull starts followed by the warming sun as the day proceeded. Rain and mud were the worst enemies, and—upon such days—it was a major task in the evenings for mum (or granny) to dry out our clothes, tidy up the boots, and make us ready for the next day's hard work.

I remember when Peem and I picked tatties at Boddin Farm, we stayed with Auntie Jean at her Smiddy (blacksmith's) Cottage, and we arrived in the tattie field one morning to be told that it was "ower weet for pickin' the day." Hurray—it was now a day to play on the swing in grandad's big shed. In those days, home phones were a rarity and mobile phones non-existent. Thus information had to be spread by word of mouth, so the farmer had to find ways to contact his work force.

There was always fun while on the tattie field. Sometimes this could take the form of "rotten" tatties being jokingly thrown around, or scaring the lassies (and mums) with a wee live mouse that had been dug up out of its home and found scurrying around. I always thought of Robert Burns' poem when a mouse was dug up. What a shame for a poor wee innocent mouse! Of course, the grieve soon put a stop to any over-zealous pranks and reminded us that we were there to work, not play. Obviously, there were no toilets in the middle of a large tattie field, giving rise to some embarrassment for the girls and mums who had to try and find some greater privacy.

While picking tatties which were laid out "cleanly" on the ground by the digger, there was always a danger that a few tatties were accidentally buried and not picked. The grieve had the answer: "harrowing". This practice was carried out after the entire field had been dug up and picked. The harrow was, effectively, a large rake around 10 feet wide and 6 feet long, with many 9 inch-long spikes or prongs pulled along behind a tractor or horse. All pickers were lined up, shoulder to shoulder, in a long wide row, and—starting at the edge of the field—the line of pickers, each carrying a basket, moved forward in a line at the same pace. A cart or bogey was stationed behind the moving line and collected filled baskets of tatties when required. This was the farmer's effective way of ensuring a "clean" pick.

A common practice in those days, prior to large storage sheds, was to store picked tatties in a pit. Always, alongside the edge of a field, where there was easy access for tractors from the road, a trench-pit—sometimes the length of a field, and approximately one foot deep—was dug, and a layer of straw laid down. Once the loaded carts and bogeys were filled, they were reversed up to the trench, and the tatties unloaded. A "pyramid" shape of tatties, about 5 or 6 feet high, was built, then covered by a 12 inch-deep thatch of straw which was subsequently covered by a 12 inch-deep "earthroof." The purpose of this was to store tatties well into the winter in a safe frost-free place until required. Looking back, I now realise that a farmer's approach to planning and dealing with the tattie harvest was quite impressive—first, there was, effectively, a clever "work-study" approach to the entire process of picking and transport. In the absence of modern-day storage facilities, tattie pits were a clever use of available resources.

"Clever grieves applied an effective management approach without any college training!"

Bonfire at the Ballaster, Westhaven (1953)

A wee poem.

Note: Sand ballast for boats had been, for many years (18th and 19th centuries?), removed from the grassy area above the high tide mark. During my years at Westhaven I never saw ballast removed. The resultant hollowed out space, by then grass-covered, was where we played football, cricket and rounders.

My sister Isobel in a white dress, playing "rounders" at the ballaster!

The black spot at the "ballaster" had been obvious all year—
It reminded me of the night amid great fun and cheer
We remembered Mr Fawkes
When a fire was lit by a coastguard with a match from a box.

The task of building the intended monument of fire
Had begun in warm summer days, when someone unknown, had laid down an old car tyre.
By the work of a few a mountain of debris grew,

And by September the infant bonfire was ready for the adults to view.

"You need a lot more than what you've got there, boys," we were told.
Thus, we set off on a mission so intensely bold
To fetch and carry a collection of any unwanted piece—
Old chairs, fish boxes, carpets... in fact, anything that neighbours could release.

Excitement grew and with a month to go
The coastguards, with a learned eye, advised us the pile was still too low.
Yet somehow, mysteriously, the collection began to grow.
Farmers and fishers brought mighty loads, and we dreamed of the biggest-ever bonfire show.

Railway sleepers, trees and an old mattress appeared
And hoisted on top in an old armchair was an effigy of Guy the 'un-revered'
The moment came when mums and dads (and even lassies)
Gathered around the dark monumental stack of impending flaming gasses...

Alas, the rain started, and dreams of a glowing blaze were shattered
How to get the flames going was all that mattered
To the rescue came a Coastie wi a can o' petrol
"Stand back" he cried, as he splashed on the magic oil.

As parents pulled wee ones away from the stack
The Coastguard called out, "I have a match ready, so stand well back!"
With a "whoomph" there was an instant circle of fire
And suddenly we had our longed-for bonfire.

With the money we earned on our evenings of guising
We set off favourite rockets and watched them rising
Through the sparks and flames they took off into flight
And added something special to that remarkable night.

With Guy Fawkes gone and the fireworks depleted,

The roaring inferno was dimming and with bodies well-heated
We set off for home after a memorable conflagration
Having taken part in the annual fireworks celebration.

Remember, remember, the 5th November
Gunpowder treason and plot
There's no reason why our "ballaster" bonfires should be forgot.

Unlike Mr Fawkes' plan our bonfire was all aflame
While Parliament buildings remained tall—
Guy to the gallows did go with shame.

"Bonfire nights were special!"

Guising in Carlogie Road, 1951/53

"That's the trouble—posh fowk ken the words o' songs and poems better than we do!"

My family lived at 4 Anchor Place, Admiral Street, and Billy Coffin (Coffey), with younger brother Ronnie, lived with his family just around the corner at Woodruff Place, Tayside Street. Most of our Halloween "guising" was done in Westhaven and along Tayside Street, but once we plucked up courage we also ventured over the other side of the railway line to a "different" world. We visited homes of well-known neighbours near home, but such was our drive to finance our fireworks ambitions that

The ballaster as it appears in more recent times.

The coastguard lookout tower at Westhaven. In the background is the roof of the terrace of villas which coastguard officers' families enjoyed.

we, cheekily but in a well-behaved way, set out to pastures new. Below is my slightly dramatised version of one of our Hallowe'en escapades:

"How much do we ha'e in our tinny, Robbie?" asked Coffey with expectation.

"I'm no' sure. It's heavy now, but I would guess... maybe about £2 10/- (£2.50p)."

"That's 'cos we got a load o' pennies twa hooses ago," added my brother, Peem.

"We'll stop and count when we get to the next lampy," I suggested. "Hold on to my neep, Coffey, while I tip oot our collection on the pavee." After a quick count, we found that the total was £2.12.2 (About £2.60).

"It's still early, boys," said Coffey, "and we ha'e hooses further up the hill to get to. Let's keep goin'. We need at least three quid so we can get a £1 each to buy oor squibs at Woody's," he enthused.

"Let's try the bigger hooses like we did last year," Peem urged. "We got plenty money there."

"Right, let's keep going!" I said. "But remember, Coffey; dinna forget your words o' 'Tae a Moose'!"

"Aye, okay… but you stuttered ow'r the words o' 'Doon in the Glen'!"

"Come on, you twa—stop arguing," Peem pleaded.

After our exciting adventure into "foreign territory," and emboldened by our self-proclaimed extraordinarily good performances, we walked—via the Smokey Brig—back to Admiral Street and had a giggle about our experiences. In good spirits, we reached the lampy nearest Anchor Place and sat around in a huddle on the pavee and tipped out the can.

"£3.14.6 (£3.72)!" I gasped. Screaming with delight, we set about dividing our collection, which we found amounted to £1.4.10 each (just over £1.20).

"It was better this year for all of us being dressed as pirates!" remarked Peem, and I suggested we should do the same next year.

"Aye, I didna like being dressed up as a witch last year," Coffey moaned.

Excitedly, we started to make plans about which fireworks we each planned to buy at Woody's newsagent shop, where Mr Wood—in his usual enthusiastic Halloween way—spread a vast selection of fireworks over his wide and cluttered counter, which was about the size of a big door. We each had our favourites. Coffey could never resist buying lots of "Barkin' Doggies."

"You just like to fleg the lassies," Peem piped up. "I'm going to buy more of the bigger rockets this year," he added while stuffing his share of coins into his pocket.

"That's 'cos you're aye dreaming about goin' tae the moon," responded Coffey. "What'll you get, Robbie?" he enquired curiously.

"Oh, more Roman candles and Catherine wheels this year, I think."

"Ye big sissy, Robbie! Tryin' tae be posh this year?" My wee brother said with a dangerous cheek.

"I'll be sending you up on one of your rockets, Peem, if you're no' careful," I replied.

The wind seemed to become colder and, to avoid the chill blast, we made our way to the beach hut at the ballaster where we sat with our neep lanterns flickering around us. There, in that spooky spot with the roar of the incoming tide echoing around us, we looked back over the daring adventure to perform our party pieces at Carlogie Road. Our general view was that we had been more successful because we had spent more time practising the words of our songs and poems.

"It's worth walkin' ower the railway line to get to the posh fowk at Carlogie Road," Peem observed thoughtfully.

"Aye, but the problem is they're awfi clever fowk," added Coffey. "They ken the words o' our sangs and poems mair than we do!"

"It's a lot better when we're invited into the hoose," my brother added.

"Aye, we're oot o' the cald but we seem tae get mair questions," I reflected.

"That man at number seven asked us if we knew where Halloween started," Coffey remarked. "And you said just after the war, Peem! You were well off the mark, 'cos the man said it started in Scotland and Ireland in the year 3 BC."

"Aye, but Peem did'na say *which* war," I said in defence of my brother. "I did'na ken Halloween was halfway between the summer solstice and the winter equinox."

"I thought it was because of Guy Fawkes," said Coffey.

"No, that wifie in the big white hoose said Bonfires had been burned at Halloween for many centuries, and had nothing to do wi' the 5th o' November."

"Remember the auld man who lived alone. He said he was very pleased to see us. He was the only one to gi'e us a half crown!"

"He was the one that told us that dookin' for apples in this country was invented by the Romans when they brought apples from Italy in the 1st Century. Something to do wi' Pamona, the goddess o' the harvest."

"I liked that clever man," added Coffey. "But it was the minister who told us about the history of the word 'Halloween.' Something aboot the church starting off on All Souls Day and Halloween was the evening before 'All Hallow Tide,' or something like that."

"But what I still dinna understand," said Peem, "Is why do we have to dae a party piece at all?"

"Well, remember what the skinny woman wi' the posh voice said. Long ago, the people who went around the doors and giving prayers to ones who had lost a relative were rewarded for their kindness."

"Jings! Is that why we go through a' that torture?" he muttered.

"That was funny when the mannie wi' the thick specs asked Peem if he knew why he put a light inside his spooky neep wi' a carved face."

"I ken, Peem—you shouldn'a hae said it was to frighten yer granny!"

"Well, now we know it's because the ugly face is to scare awa' evil spirits, and the light inside is meant to mean a trapped spirit is trying to get out."

"Who was it that said his grandad told him about kail-pulling?"

"It was the old farmer-looking man, who said his grandad showed him how to have a competition fightin' wi' kail roots."

"Aye, the winner would get the best-looking lassie in the village!"

"He was the one who told us Rabbie Burns wrote aboot Halloween superstitions."

"Well, it's getting' late," Coffee pointed out. "My mum will think we've been kidnapped up Carlogie Road."

"Well, isn't it amazing? We had nae idea that we were daein' things that had been goin' on for centuries," reflected Peem.

"You see? Ye get mair than pennies when you go guising tae clever fowk."

Guisin' in the 1950s—could you beat that?

Caravan Holiday

"Dad! Dad! Robert's fa'n doon a well!"

Mum and dad didn't have money to take us away on an annual holiday, but—fortunately for me—both parents were keen "get up and go" people. Exciting visits by bus to my mother's parents at Woodside Croft, Dunninald or to see my other gran and grandad in Montrose were quite regular, but with no car those were our only trips away as a family.

Somehow, when I was about 8-or 9-years old mum and dad discovered a family holiday offer they could afford. The arrangement they found was that a man in Dundee, running his own caravan hire business, would come to pick us all up in his car at Admiral Street and drive us to his caravan in the hills behind Dunkeld. It must have been July or August, perhaps in 1949—the year Isobel was about to start school. An historic family moment, perhaps when mum would finally find all her children were finally off her attentive hands at home.

The exciting day finally arrived when the biggest black shiny car that I'd ever seen in Westhaven pulled up outside Anchor Place, and we all clambered aboard. I still remember the warm leather smell inside the luxurious vehicle. Yes, this was quite a big event in our lives—a run ('hurl') in a car! Some 50 miles later, after sitting quietly on our best behaviour and gazing out at unusual places, we found ourselves at a flat spot in the hills. It wasn't a caravan park, but there were two or three parked caravans well-spaced in the grassy area which seemed to be surrounded by lush green ferns. While mum and dad were appreciating the view, we immediately climbed aboard our allocated caravan to check out the features of our holiday home. The smell of gas was noticeable, but the bunks and layout were exciting and something quite like another world.

During the week we had walks all around the area, exploring woods and spotting a great variety of birds hitherto never seen by us. Early examples of a living creature new to us

The man and the big black shiny car, with our holiday caravan in the background. Dad is on the left in the photo. From L to R: James (Peem), Isobel and Robbie.

was to find sunbathing lizards which suddenly darted down gaps in the roadside stone walls. The freedom of running around in new surroundings was full of fun and adventure. Isobel loved making "jam," as she called it, by collecting rowan berries and filling glass jars with imagined "rowan jam" in water. Peem and I discovered a new, exciting experience: catching frogs! The area seemed to be a happy breeding place for the biggest ever population of the lively hoppers. We discovered a small, fenced-off area provided the most prolific breeding ground. We became so infatuated by the exciting finds that, to this day, I recall the event clearly, for within the fenced-off patch was a large stone slab measuring about three feet square. It seemed innocuous enough, but—in a moment of excitement as I darted over it—to my horror, the stone suddenly gave way. Unnoticed by me was that the stone was cracked. With supreme luck, my young weight was not sufficient to push the broken stone down, otherwise I would have fallen down the space.

As I sat there with my legs trapped and the slab finely balanced and wobbling, I could peer through the gap and see—very many feet below—the surface of a water-filled well. Unable to move, I started screaming, and Peem ran off shouting "Dad!" at the top of his voice. After what seemed an age, an adult grabbed me from behind and clutched me under their armpits while some men—including my father—acted together to slide the stone away. Obviously Peem and I should not have ventured inside the fence, but there was no sign referring to dangers and the slab was not in one piece. All I recall is not sleeping for many nights due to the constant reminder of what the scenario might have been if I had slipped many feet into the well in my pre-swimming days with nothing to hold onto to stay afloat.

Another surprise awaited—this time, a happy one. It seems today it would have been an easy journey, but in 1949 it was quite an adventure for my dad's parents who decided to visit us during our stay, which must have been quite an exhausting trip. From their home in Montrose, they took a train to Perth and then another train to Dunkeld, followed by a walk from the railway station up to the caravan. Looking back, I think they must have been in their sixties, but with heavy old-fashioned suits and coats their gruelling trek to us must have been quite tiring. Quite a feat to plan trains to and from Dunkeld, but at least at no cost as grandad enjoyed free rail travel obtained by his long service on the railways.

The week was a wonderful example of how mum and dad, over the years, introduced us to an outdoor life. It fitted with my Cubs camping experiences, and demonstrated how it was possible to have a family holiday in new surroundings. I have loving admiration for that introduction to explore new places. A wonderful holiday with an unforgettable, scary tale to tell. I'm still left admiring my mum and dad and their marvellous love of camping, as well as their energy to explore.

"Well, well, well—what a lucky escape!"

My Trips to Lunan Bay, Boddin, Usan, Craig, Montrose, and Sunday Family Gatherings at the Croft.

"On Boxing Day we'll get the 10 o'clock bus at Swannie's Café and take some Christmas cordial to Granny and Grandad at Woodside!"

Lunan Bay and Boddin

On the coast, about five miles east of Arbroath, is the three-mile-long crescent-shaped, sandy Lunan Bay. I have often idly wondered if the "Lun" in Lunan had anything to do with the crescent moon? But as it happens, there is a better explanation. "Lunan" originates from two Gaelic words meaning "River of Two Lochs": namely Forfar Loch and Rescobie. I have seen documentary evidence that there was a plan, many years ago, to create a canal linking the river Lunan and the lochs to aid transport of fish supplies to inland Forfar. At the western end of the bay is the original salmon fishing village of Ethiehaven. With the death of the salmon fishing industry in the 1970s and '80s, the quaint custom-built properties of the 1800s are now utilised as private holiday homes. Although stake-net fishing would have been carried out along the bay, there is evidence of boats having been used at Ethiehaven.

Parking a car at the nearby Ethiebeaton Farmyard, it is a fifteen-minute walk down to the village. As a young man, my mother's brother Jim worked as a ploughman on the farm prior to becoming grieve at Ethiebeaton Farm, near Monifieth. Red Castle ruins at Lunan are so dilapidated, they are now unsafe to inspect at close range. Robert the Bruce donated the castle in 1328 to the Earl of Ross. In a book my mother gave me about the history of Dunninald Castle (where she worked as a maid and cook), I read there were serious rivalries between the two castle families.

My father's father was Signalman, then Station Master, at Lunan Railway Station, which served the village and most likely the commercial salmon industry. My father and his siblings all lived there and attended school at Inverkeiler, about three miles away beside the main Arbroath/Montrose road. My mother's father was grieve at Boddin farm at the east end of Lunan Bay. Salmon fishing boats were very active at Boddin, and the original underground "ice store" is still in place. There are also signs of where lobsters and partons (edible crabs) were cooked outdoors. It's very easy to this day to imagine the industry and hustle and bustle of the salmon fishing world at Boddin.

What is still of interest are the remnants of the close-by limekilns building where, from the late 18th Century onwards, imported limestone was burned to produce lime dust to spread on farm fields in the area. At the nearby "Elephant Rock" formation is an interesting walled burial ground containing the deceased from Dunninald Castle and the area. In 1914, my mother was born in one of the nearby farm cottages.

Usan

"Ye'd better be careful—His Lordship's agent will around the morn to collect dues."

This was probably a more active fishing port than both Ethiehaven and Boddin. There has been, up to the present day, fishing and lobster creel fishing. A railway line existed until the Beeching cuts came in the early 1970s. Positioned as it is, Usan was also a coastguard base.

The entire coastline of Scotland is, of course noted for its fishing industry, and the wide sweeping sandy bays from Barry in Angus to St Cyrus were famed for salmon fishing. Each settlement collectively must have been a massive provider of fish for both local and London markets—a sad demise.

The Earl of Dalhousie of Panmure House, near Carnoustie, through his agents collected 'dues' from the many fisherfolk operating from Monifieth to Montrose.

Craig (near Ferryden)

"They are fishers and farmers in this neck of the woods!"

To understand the work and population in this part of the county, one must imagine the area of Craig and Ferryden prior to the building of the road bridge link to Rossie Island and the imposing railway bridge nearby. With only a small ferry boat link to Rossie Island and Montrose, it must have been an isolated coastal area south of the River South Esk. Montrose had developed as an important North Sea port, and provided a valuable economic centre for the area.

As a young person, I picked up the vibes that "Ferrydeners" were quite insular people who didn't mix much with locals. They were fisher folk, and kept themselves to themselves. Craig and the area of Rossie Braes, on the other hand, were inhabited by farming people. My mother told me she walked three miles daily to Craig village school from Boddin—with bare feet in the summertime! Hardy people!

Craig Church is interesting in that it has no graveyard. Only a few Dunninald Castle family members are buried there. The Craig and Ferryden dead were buried in Rossie Island graveyard. I suspect the financing of the church origins was met by Dunninald Castle families. My parents were married in the church, and I was christened there in December 1940. One can only imagine the "friendly" rivalry between the farming people of Craig and the fisher fowk o' Ferryden.

Montrose

"Yes – Montrose has a touch o' class about it."

In my opinion, Montrose is the best-presented town in Angus. With its classical High School, museum buildings, and the elegant town centre and church spires, it stands out above the rest. The spacious parks and statues in the town add to the dignified grace. As a market town and thriving seaport supporting the county, it was obviously an economic jewel that stood out. Only Forfar's geographic central position and its farming and jute businesses claimed its right as a significant market county town.

Gatherings at Woodside Croft

"Watch oot! Your dad's driven into the midden!"

You will have noticed my favoured bias towards Montrose as a town, and this obviously has its base from my many family visits. I recall, especially, Montrose-based bakers' vans which came around the countryside with products, and the many references made by my grandparents to trips into town—and especially my grandfather's Friday market-day visits.

Farming community families liked to gather in groups at weekends, and also special weekends or seasonal holidays. I suspect that in earlier years end-of-term times would have been a significant occasion for family gatherings. My parents enjoyed taking us to visit the Croft quite regularly. We travelled very happily by Bluebird bus, stopping at the White Inn bus stop and walking a mile to the cottage. Invariably, we would meet other families—the Duthies from the Smiddy down the road, and the Taylor families from Ethiebeaton (Monifieth), Aberdeen and Ferryden. Those gatherings were unplanned

—they just seemed to "happen." No phones were involved!

The Duthies and Monifieth Taylors talked about farming, and the oldest uncle I had (Uncle Will) was a policeman in Aberdeen, and was the only uncle with a car— so other uncles surrounded him to hear about his car's plusses and minuses. My dad learned to drive Uncle Will's car in the farmyard, with near-disastrous results at the midden.

The Taylors from Ferryden were unique, for Uncle George—an "outsider"—had married a Ferryden lady who we never met, but his daughters joined us. I enjoyed playing with my cousins on the shed swing, looking after the pigs and hens, and sometimes helping to cut the lawn or hedges. Time went past so quickly, and I will never know how much food Granny and Grandad must have provided for around twenty hungry travellers. We enjoyed those extended family gatherings, and I gained a good deal of "unwitting learning."

Clyde Steamers

"Look up to that tenement block—that's what they call a 'Hingy Oot'!"

So far in my recollections, I have made mention of the many aspects of life and living where my parents' care and attention to me and my sisters and brother were thoughtful, modern in their day, and paid for by their careful management of their limited income. Yet, they did a huge amount which must have been possible only by their own sacrifices. Holidays to a caravan in Dunkeld and a memorable holiday to Jersey (transport courtesy of British Rail), and financing my Boy Scout camping trips, are just a few additional expenses above the good wholesome food and the constantly updated clothing they provided, along with a regular churchgoing background.

During the summer of 1952, mum and dad took us to Greenock to spend a week with mum's sister Annie and husband Charlie. It was our first experience in Greenock, and we had been looking forward to the rail journey (free as part dad's pay package) with a change of train in Glasgow for another train to Greenock. That part of the journey was of special interest to our family, since another uncle was a train driver on that branch line which terminated at Gourock.

A holiday in Greenock presented a view of an entirely different world for me. The lively, almost intense, energy and industry which could be sensed emanating from the shipyards and engineering workshops was mesmerising. There always seemed to be the constant background noise of hammering and riveting, interspersed with ships' horns and the incessant road traffic moving materials around.

Uncle Charlie worked for a company called Kincaid, which—we learned—specialised in manufacturing ships' engines. From the lounge window of his "industrial smoke coated" black and lofty situated semi-detached villa, he enthusiastically pointed out to me and my brother everything that was happening all over the river: that ship is doing that, or this—that tug is getting ready to move that boat—that ship is laid up—and that giant ship is the *Empress of Canada,* waiting to be filled with emigrants to Canada paying £10 for a ticket. His list of on-going, non-stop commentary was breathtaking. He seemed to know every element of Greenock's shipping and ship-building industry which, in those pre-television days, was remarkable.

For many parents, a week in Greenock would have been sufficient, but—being the energetic and adventurous people they were—mum and dad enhanced the holiday by arranging sailing trips on McBraynes steamers. The thrill of being up on deck, watching the coastline and shipping around us, was always captivating. But to go down into the ship's engine room and see the workings of the paddle steamers was exhilarating and transfixing. The engineering, the power, and the sheer majesty of the workings was entrancing.

We sailed to Largs, Dunoon, Kilchattan Bay, Millport, Rothesay, and the Kyles of Bute. Each port had its own architecture and personality and, if we were not disembarking, we stood mesmerised as we watched the procedure of the steamer coming alongside

Enjoying an ice cream on a sailing day out on the Clyde. Note the casual dress of the time!

the jetty. We were in Scotland, and yet we felt transported to another world.

It's strange how some aspects of a holiday stand out. Greenock is built on high, sloping ground with terraced housing and steep streets stretching down to the busy shipbuilding areas on the banks of the River Clyde. In 1952, there seemed to be massive four- or five-storey tenement blocks dominating the town. Signs of its industrial background were evident in its blackened stone architecture. On one sunny evening, while out for a walk, my uncle pointed out to us the local habit of having what he called "a hingy oot."

When we asked him to explain, he replied: "Look up at the tenement windows. Do you see? The windows are all opened, and people are sitting at their windows enjoying the sunny evening and the view across the river."

Sure enough, when we looked at the entire scene, the building was populated by people perched at their window with elbows resting on the windowsill while enjoying the evening sun. I remember thinking at the time it was akin to birds quietly roosting on perches enjoying a sunny evening.

On a more sombre note, another memory was the number of derelict bomb sites in Greenock. Uncle Charlie told us the town was hit badly by German bombers during World War 2. It was the growth of the pink blossom plant Rosebay Willowherb which dominated the bomb sites, and it remains in my mind to this day. The Cross of Lorraine naval monument on the crest of the hill seemed for me to resonate perfectly with the town's massive ship building and wartime history.

"Lovely day for a sail doon the watter!"

A Murray family day at the beach.
Robbie is shown at the centre of the photo.

CHAPTER 3

Carnoustie

A Split Toon

"We're a' Jock Tamson's bairns! (But there were some differences...)"

It is a slightly sensitive topic to talk about Carnoustie being a "split toon," arising from the quirky geography of being a "lang toon." It was in my young days—and it is, perhaps, still today—a town of two parts, although each part continues to show great respect to one another. It is not an issue today—we are all equal, and we are "a' Jock Tamson's bairns"—but it was a town of some contrasts over a hundred years ago.

I should start by saying I have no doubt at all that in my past, and as now, I am as comfortable anywhere in the town, but over the many years industry and commerce have dictated how life has panned out.

The embryonic town determined how things would unfold. Firstly, the Barry Burn, I suggest, is the striking feature which determined the town's development. Although very early maps show sparse dwellings and wells which must have helped determine location of houses, it is the Barry Burn which must have tempted early industrial and economic development at the west end of the town. (It is worth noting that another industrial development did take place where there was a water supply, and that was the bleachfield at Craigmill Burn. It is interesting to promote a theory that had the Craigmill Burn been more "influential" than the Barry Burn then perhaps we would have witnessed more industrial development at the east end of the town. However, my guess is that the raised ground up Carlogie Road and Queen Street would have offered preferred private property development.) One may have thought the railway, when established in 1838, would have promoted even more economic growth at the west end, thus siting the railway station at that end. However, the railway station was developed at the east end. Why would that happen? Was this because less space was available at the west end? And why would the dusty coal yard and sidings be sited at the east end? Was it possibly the fact that influential people living in good quality residential housing wanted the railway station there?

Thus, even more growth of quality Victorian properties were built at the east end, and so the divide began to become more evident. (What is unusual is that, with a prevailing west wind, industrial growth would be expected in the east end of town—but again, I think the Barry Burn was the defining factor.) The labour force for the industrial end of the town therefore was housed in the west. In time, Carnoustie Burgh and Forfarshire County Council saw fit to build the earliest council house properties at the west end—in Victoria Street and Charles Street—followed later by pre-fabs and the 'flower streets': Primrose, Shamrock, Rose and Thistle, again to help working people at the west end.

As I grew up in the town, I became increasingly aware of signs or evidence of the "split." Almost without exception, all children at the east end displayed more wealth in sporting equipment, greater sporting opportunities, had better bicycles, and had parents who, mostly, owned cars. Spare time interests such as music instruction, model boat or aeroplane building were evident, and certainly all would—after the 11+ exams (prior to the High School being built in 1974)—go on to study at Arbroath High School.

In my own case my family had, by chance, luckily ended up living at the east end—albeit on the "different" side of the railway line. So yes, privilege in the east was evident. Apart from the distinctions drawn by the siting of the railway station, the establishment of

Newton Panbride Church in the east and St Stephen's and the Old Parish Churches in the centre had some significance. There was no church at the west end. (Note: Panbride Country Church served the country areas around the east end and both Barry Churches—east and west—served the village, although I believe the Barry parish extends as far east as West Path, which must have attracted local families to attend Barry East Church (and Barry School?). There was, however, a church near Thistle Street, but it did not remain there long. Thus, the social economic divide became more pronounced.

Carnoustie's Economy

"Carnoustie: a pulsating wee toon with a totally self-sufficient economic history. The 1950s and 60s were probably the most productive decades."

In the preceding section, "A Split Toon", I referred to some elements of the town's industry and, in this one, I'd like to mention some of the more prominent enterprises which sustained and enhanced growth of the town and district.

Barry Mill, one of four mills in earlier centuries up to the mid-20th Century, had been an important part of the area since the 15th Century. Prior to the end of the 19th Century, cottage-based weaving would have provided stable employment for local people. Along with fishing and farming, those functions must have provided the basics for economic survival.

Carnoustie was not untouched by the gradual arrival of the industrial revolution, and other business opportunities would arise. (Numbers employed, noted as follows, are estimates based on anecdotal evidence.) Up to my teen years, I was aware of the SAI (Scottish Agricultural Industries), located near the railway at the south end of Victoria Street. (In earlier times, a Vitriol Works carried out a similar function.) My understanding is that the business—employing around 40 people—provided chemical feeds for agricultural purposes. It was nicknamed "the Tanny," and permanently gave off an unpleasant smell. Following the dismantling of "the Tanny," the site was used by Paul's Malt, a barley malting company. Houses have now been built on the site, suggesting there had been no detrimental impact of the ground.

Beyond the south end of James Street was the Anderson Grice foundry, which found great prominence in the engineering world both in the UK and abroad. One example was a giant saw-blade which had to be transported by road to Middlesborough in England, and a chocolate boiling kettle apparatus which was especially made for a company in Turkey. Around 1906, the company also pioneered car manufacture with production of the *Dalhousie* car. The foundry, with approximately 150/200 employees, presented a range of engineering opportunities for local school leavers, and was a breeding ground for Merchant Navy engineers, as well for draughtsmen and pattern-makers. An essential requirement for industries located in that area was the existence of a railway siding of the main line. The railway was opened in 1838, and a siding was created quite soon afterwards.

The development of the highly successful and supportive James Smieton & Son linen works, established 1842, effectively put the process of cottage linen weaving industry under one roof, and was also based alongside the railway. At its height with 400 looms, W.G. Grant's (latter day owners) employed up to 500/600 personnel. Another organisation, established in 1867, was Taymouth Linen Works—employing around 80 people and 40 looms. The existence of the nearby Barry Burn and the availability of labour living in surrounding cottages probably kickstarted early industry, and it is surprising that for a small town, then of no more than three thousand population, that such enterprises flourished.

The population during those early days was most definitely at that west end of the town. The east end of the town with its prominence of substantial stone-built villas and terraces began following the creation of the railway station 1838. In the minutes of Town Council meetings around 1899–1901, it is recorded that plans were set in motion for a railway platform to be created at the west end of the town, but this came to nothing. Likewise, around the same period there was some discussion around a plan to extend the Dundee Tram system to Carnoustie—again, to no avail, but this indicates something about the industrial "pulse" at the west end of the town and the growth of the local working population.

Entrepreneurs in those early times must have seen the prospects aided by available local labour, a water supply, railway access, and the nearby toll road linking the east coast towns and especially the nearby city of Dundee, which would have provided supportive skilled trades. Added to the sizeable operations described above was Winter's shoe factory, located at the south end of Park Avenue and employing around 200 people. Although positioned near the railway, there is no evidence of an adjacent railway siding, but again the owners must have been assured of a labour supply and good transport links. Winter's shoe factory closed, and the building was, in time, occupied by East Coast Enterprises—a Lockwood's canning company with links to fruit and vegetable canning in East Anglia. Employing around 100 people, this ran successfully for several years until the business was transferred to the company's sister plant in Forfar.

Somehow, a fraction of the shoe manufacturing trade in the town survived, with the establishment of a small Saxone factory engaging 20-40 employees located behind the Regal Cinema in premises now occupied (in 2025) by the British Legion when they moved their base from Kinloch Street (almost opposite the 19th Hole)—previously a fish and chip shop. It is interesting to note that Carnoustie also had, in the period 1860s–1920s, Scroggie's shoe factory, engaging around 50 employees.

Craigmill Burn served as a crucial element in the setting up of the Bleachfield business. The remains of the dam and sluice at Craigmill Den, and the creation of a water channel to fill the two extensive reservoirs situated near Easthaven Road, indicate investment to ensure that the bleachfield could operate. No doubt it provided an essential part of the linen industry, and again must have relied upon a supply of labour—perhaps from local farming families.

Carnoustie seems always to have had a clever and inventive source of industry. I have read of Mr Ferrier, the boat-builder, who created a channel from the sea to his premises just next door to the 19th Hole in Ferrier Street. Obviously, prior to the erection of the Beach Café and tennis courts, the channel must have connected to his premises by a route where—today—the railway bridge at the south end of Ferrier Street is located.

The town had a reputation for growing good carrots in the sandy soil and, in 1898, a plan was submitted to the Burgh Council by Mr George Gibson to build a factory to can carrots. Later, in that same cannery building, a jam factory was run by Mr Mackay, whose jams became a very well-known brand up to the 1950s, '60s, and '70s. These days, the sandy field which accommodated the jam factory's fruit barrels is occupied by the Police Station and police housing. I recall marram grass grew between the large oak barrels which were stored in that sandy field. As a message boy with Wm Low & Co., I vividly remember delivering large quantities of sugar, lemons and eggs during non-jam-making periods, when Mr Mackay produced Lemon Curd.

The golfing world boasted similar adventurous business spirit when Walter and David Hewitt, in the period 1895–1925, designed and made golf clubs and manufactured advanced designed golf balls. Simpsons' likewise developed a golf club-making business, and employed as many as 20 employees.

The "service" support functions of gas works, laundry, and retail added significantly to the number of available jobs in the town. The brave attempts by Carnoustie's entrepreneurs demonstrates a town with people who had ideas and innovation for commerce and engineering.

In 1901 there were two slaughterhouses at Ravensby Feus, one at Westhaven, one in Maule Street, and another in Yeaman Street. Eventually only one (and the last) operated during the early/mid part of the 1900s on the west side of Lochend Road. When the railway line opened on 6th August 1838, so too were the stations at Carnoustie and Easthaven, and it is likely that the extensive sidings at Station Road were also completed then or soon afterwards. Over the years the sidings have probably served many purposes, but two I am aware of were off-loading coal and on-loading sugar beet for the sugar beet factory at Cupar, Fife.

Coal merchants in the town I recall were Taylor Bros., Smith, Hood and Sons, and Thomas Muir, Son & Paton. Coal was sacked at the sidings, and horse-drawn, flat-bed wagons delivered bags of coal around the town. As a boy, I was allowed by one of the coalmen, Dod (George) Leslie, to stand in the coal-yard and watch him weigh up hundred-weight bags of coal and obtain a glimpse of his horse, which was kept in the yard. Dod wore a heavy, studded leather back protector to assist him in safely carrying hundredweight bags of coal on his back—a very tiring job!

In the autumns of the 1950s and '60s, when sugar beet was harvested, local farmers transported trailer-loads of raw sugar beet to the railway sidings. Beets are similar in size to turnips, but whiter and more pointed in appearance. Loads were weighed then tipped into railway wagons, and what appealed to me was the tidy way in which the mounds of beets on the wagon were built almost in pyramid-like shape, with the top layer of beets packed 'tail-down'.

From my study of grocery trade subjects, I knew the destination for the loads was the Cupar sugar beet processing factory, which I had visited as part of my studies. We were taken through the entire process from washing beets to the boiling procedure, when sugar crystals are formed. My most vivid recollection is that it was one man (the sugar boiler) who made the decision to stop boiling when he, alone, judged the correct size of the crystals having examined a sample on a glass slide.

Paraffin, Gas, and Electricity

"Quite a few wee changes during my lifetime, mum!"

It is to my good fortune that I have never been "called up" to fight in a war. I enjoyed a period of full employment, and am in receipt of my employer's pension scheme supplemented by my state pension. I have witnessed great advances in medical science, motor car development, improved motorway systems, and generally advances in science, technology, and engineering which have seen great improvements in so many ways. Domestic lighting and heating improvements have provided safer and healthier living conditions. As a boy, I recall we had an open coal fireplace and used stand-alone paraffin heaters—sometimes one which could be moved from room to room, with associated safety risks. Later, heating was produced by oil-filled electric heaters and various types of convector heaters. Of course, the normal fireplace—where logs or coal was burned—was the standard main form of heating, but usually only in the main living room space and some bedrooms. I recall my mother transferring a shovel full of burning coal upstairs to my bedroom fireplace in order that I had peace and quiet to study during my night-class days. What a health and safety risk that was! Today, heating is by electricity, solar panels, gas or oil central heating boilers, and only in specialised custom-built properties are there any open coal fires. Enclosed log burners are also now available.

Lighting in the first cottage I lived in was by paraffin lamps and when we moved to the flat in Anchor Place, lighting was by gas mantle. I recall the momentous day when electricity was installed—suddenly we had on/off lighting in an instant, as well as the prospect of an electric cooker, oven, moveable heaters, and the ability to plug in devices. The accent in 2025 is for low-cost, climate-friendly systems of heating and lighting. A good example of this is the siting of solar panels on rooftops, and new-built council homes are now routinely fitted with panels.

Golf at Carnoustie

"Look, boys—you're holding yer clubs pally handed!" cried the railway signalman.

In my tales, I must not ignore the subject of golf, which has been played on Carnoustie links since the 16th century—placing the area and eventually the town on the world golfing map. Symbols on the logo of the local heritage group "Friends of Carnoustie and District Heritage" reflect the long history of Barry, Panbride, and Easthaven with Carnoustie, denoted by the "Dibble Tree" and by crossed golf clubs.

My first experiences of playing the game go back to around 1951 and 1952, when Peem and I played on the Burnside course with our hickory-shaft clubs. I had blissfully—or, should I say, masochistically—enjoyed playing my boyhood golf with a white (or badly weathered) pencil golf bag complete with a "brassie" (a No.2 wood), a "cleek" (a No.2 iron) and a putter, but it was at Christmas 1951 when Santa Claus brought me a less-worn golf bag and my longed-for additional clubs, a mashie niblick (a No.7 iron) and a jigger (chipper), along with some tees and balls. I well recall my dash on that cold, white, frosty Christmas Day, sprinting to the 'ballaster' at the end of Admiral Street (Westhaven) to have a swipe at a ball with my "posh" second-hand clubs. Such was my excitement that I stupidly lost one or two of my new balls in the long-frozen grass. Strangely, in those days we used a long wooden pole with a metal "cleek" on the end to help pull "partons" (edible crabs) out of the rock crevices, and I imagined

Robbie, Isobel and Peem putting at Carnoustie with the "old" starter's box and bandstand in the background.

then that local golf club-makers used the word "cleek" as it was of a similar shape. But which came first?

My brother and I had started playing, having had no tuition. Our hickory-shafted clubs were satisfactory, and we kept them "sand-papered clean," but I recall the nuisance "cord (or horse-hair) whipping" around the head of my brassie had a habit of coming loose. Once we had our improved clubs, we enjoyed playing. We had no golfing family members and were totally reliant on our own experimental style. I recall with some mirth that one day, the signalman in the signal-box at the Victoria Street railway crossing ran down the stairs and on to the course to show us how to hold our clubs! He had observed us playing "pally-handed" (i.e. with our left hand placed below our right). "Hud yer hands like this, boys," he told us while demonstrating.

In carefree summer school holidays and evenings, we cycled from Westhaven, left our unlocked bikes against the back wall of the Burnside starter's box, paid two pennies, and stepped on to the stage of our "young laddie's" world of golf. As we improved our game, the challenges were to hit our drives from the 1st tee to a point level with the railway footbridge, try to get our tee shots over the willow trees at the 5th, and put our tee shot at the 9th on to the plateau… and, I am happy to report, those are still my challenges today! Sadly, I must report that the 5s and 6s I scored from the junior tees are not much different from my scores of today at the age of 84.

Unlike me, my brother Peem (a member of Carnoustie Golf Club) has regularly played golf—summer and winter—all his life, and still going strong aged 83. Sadly, being a workaholic exiled in England, my only claim to golf fame was that Gordon Spankie—a school classmate, who went on the win the schoolboys golf Nicoll Cup—beat me by only 5 and 4. Gordon, a well-known local golfer, went on to win Club Championships.

During our school summer holidays, we played on glorious summer mornings to our total contentment on the Burnside Course. I can still remember the background chorus of skylarks and the fresh smell of new-cut grass as if it was yesterday. What glorious recollections. My most memorable experience on the Championship golf course was to kneel in my short trousers at the edge of the 18th green, with red ants crawling up my bare legs, to witness—in 1953—the famous Ben Hogan sink his winning putt to win The Open.

Carnoustie's Summer Attractions

"Every week, there's a new crop of talent!"

It is recorded that visitors began holidaying in Carnoustie from as early as mid-19th century. Some examples were families who were able to travel from inland Angus Burghs to enjoy the sea air and salty breezes. After the town became a Burgh itself, money was raised to enhance and extend the layout of the golf course, and the area beyond the golf course known as Buddon Ness was sold to the War Department. The latter part of the 1950s was a period of great improvement in how the town was organised for summer holiday visitors.

In Victorian times Carnoustie was deemed to be "The Brighton of the North," and I have seen photos of a crowded beach and have read about the town attracting summer holiday guests many years before the First World War. There seemed to be lots of ideas: donkey rides on the beach, a mini-train, music, and variety shows. The tennis courts and putting green looked busy, as did the paddling pool, and the bandstand seemed to be in good use too. In the years immediately after the Second World War, there seemed to be very little going on but five years or so after the end of WW2 things seemed to improve—albeit that some of the early century activities mentioned above had disappeared. For several years from about 1950, when people began to think of holidays, advertising and communications of daily events throughout the summer were posted all over the town with a special "month by month" reminder of forthcoming attractions.

A Carnoustie Publicity and Development Association (PDA) was formed to attract visitors to the town by advertising the town, especially around the Central Belt of Scotland, and listing all accommodation available in hotels, boarding houses, and private dwellings in the town. I remember Bill Cumming ran the Association at 22 High Street, next door to the Municipal Offices. His remit seemed to include arranging events in the town throughout the summer.

During the 1950s, while cycling around on my message bike and later working in Wm Low's grocery shop, I was aware of the excitement each summer. The hanging flower baskets on lampposts were watered regularly by council workers (the "scaffies") watering from a big barrel on a flat-bed lorry. Wooden billboards measuring about 3 feet by 12 inches wide were placed throughout the town, and each month a poster of every event was glued on. Every shop in the town was busy, and there was a real "buzz." In those days, each shop had its windows washed, and owners brushed their section of the pavement. There was a real pride in appearance. High Street and Dundee Street enjoyed a constant all-summer high "footfall."

Events and competitions were many and varied: putting, sand building, midnight dookin', bonny baby competitions, talent-spotting night, granny and baby competitions, along with races and games organised by an "Uncle". This was always the first name of a male university student whose job it was to run those events. For example, "Uncle George," who happened—for one or two years—to be George Soutar. Thursday evening was "Talent Show" night—open to any participant in certain age groups. Friday evenings were teenage dance nights, when the Beach Hall was packed with dancers and "jivers" (the new "rock and roll" dance!)—the highlight being that when the lights were dimmed, the big crystal ball revolved, casting atmospheric coloured dappled light around the hall. Say no more! At the end of each week, the first thing that occupied the minds of both boys and girls of the town was to see what the next crop of "holidaying talent" looked like.

Each Friday afternoon and evening, taxis were lined up the length of Station Road to take the Central Belt families to their preferred holiday accommodation; be it a private home, guest house, or hotel. Each year my mum had families from Falkirk and Grangemouth, who came for many successive years to Westhaven. It was commonplace in private homes for a holidaying mum, dad, and two children to be accommodated in one bedroom, and the visitors ate with the host family.

In 1951, I arrived home from my Scout Camp to find an unknown lady standing and cooking something at my mum's cooker. I didn't recognise her, but she explained that my mum had been held up at her part-time job and had asked if she would cook my meal. That was my introduction to Mrs Taylor, who had arrived from Falkirk that day to holiday for two weeks in our house along with her husband and sons Charles (10) and Ian (8). That Taylor family returned year after year for the next eight years, and thereafter parents regularly met up when visiting each other's homes. Both sets of parents have now passed away, but I still occasionally meet up with Charles.

Following that first holiday in 1951, Mr Taylor passed on good words to his sister, Mrs Christie, from Grangemouth, who in turn began holidaying with her husband and children Mary (10) and Gilbert (8). A similar pattern of friendship developed with the Christie family, and I still occasionally meet up with Mary and regularly with the Christie grandchildren (who, amazingly enough, are now highly-acclaimed independent publishers with whom I had the good fortune of having my *Grocer's Boy* books published starting in 2018.) This is a wonderful example of how holidays in the 1950s were arranged, and how long-lasting friendships ensued up to the present day.

Year after year, Carnoustie's action-packed holiday programmes were repeated until, not surprisingly, in the early 1970s inexpensive holiday packages to the sun, sea and sangria of Spain and other Mediterranean countries began to lure away holiday visitors. The twenty years from around 1950 were a highlight of the post-World War family holiday boom, which enhanced many seaside towns in Scotland.

Carnoustie, since the late-19th Century and despite the trauma of two World Wars, had remained a magnet for people seeking sunshine, seaside, and wonderful entertainment. Changes in holiday patterns and the aforementioned arrival of the package holiday boom were to end Carnoustie's renowned summer holiday history, however.

"Aye, sadly Carnoustie failed to be the Malaga of the north!"

Shops

"You can buy everything you need in Carnoustie's shops!"

Carnoustie is a linear town. That is to say, geographically it is composed of a long, narrow thoroughfare. Consequently, the layout is probably quite unique—and logical, and yet illogical, when you consider the odd mix of dwelling houses. The industrial sector of the town is in the west, which is surprising given that the prevailing wind blows smoke and dust eastwards to the more affluent east end of the town. I can only guess that the proximity of the Barry Burn for water supply may have had a lot to do with it. Another factor may be that the railway station was established (1838) at the east end of the town. Was this for the professional and wealthier section of the community to settle near the railway station for their regular commuting to Dundee city and beyond? Strangely, the larger railway sidings, useful for industrial and commercial purposes, were located near to the railway station. Had that anything to do with the fact that coal for domestic use was bagged there, nearer to the wealthier end of town?

Town Councillors were aware, around the end of the 19th Century, that the working population "deserved" a railway station at the west end of the town, and applications were made to the Dundee and Arbroath Railway company. Similarly, a town council committee was formed to engage with the Dundee tram syndicate to explore the prospect of extending the tram network to Carnoustie.

It's worth noting that from the immediate post WW2 period up to the 1950s–'70s, sugar beet was loaded on wagons at the same "coal" sidings at Station Road. This long, strung-out settlement consequently had an arrangement of shops in a particular design. Despite the working population residing at the west end of the town, the High Street and The Cross were, in early days—and even more so today—positioned east of centre. Why was that? Was it simply the volume of spending power of the wealthier east end population, and nearer to the beach and beachfront?

In a way, this is a silly section for me to attempt, as the long history of shops relies on memory with some conflicting views of who and what shop was where. I am sure some statements will conflict with readers' own recollections, so I apologise in advance. I can relate only to the location of shops from detailed knowledge of the 1950s, when I was fortunate to pedal about the town delivering groceries for Wm Low & Co. Ltd., and now—with valuable help from the Auld Carnoustie Facebook Group—I can give some history of the changes which have taken place over the years. So my intention in this chapter is to refer to shops as they exist in 2024 and to give, where possible, some background history of the shops within memory of those of us who can relate to the 1940s–50s. But please be aware: I must emphasise that my information about shops is based largely on anecdotal evidence and, in some cases, only on my own recollections. Therefore, this chapter may be subject to some unavoidable errors. I'm certain I haven't got every detail correct, but hopefully this may, at least, help to stimulate discussion. It's certain I will corrected by my "heritage" friends!

What is very clear is that shops changed both ownership and uses regularly, so this is merely a "snapshot" of how things were during the period from 1940s–'50s to the present day. Those changes reflect the passing fads and fancies in life, such as wee grocer's shops becoming fast-food takeaways. Prior to providing information of shops in High Street, Dundee Street, and Barry Road, I'd like to refer to small shops in non-central areas of the town.

Non-central areas

Isolated small shops appeared around the periphery of the main shopping area, and this was more marked at the west end of the town where industrial workers resided. In addition to running a small shop, ambitious operators would benefit from buying products for their own domestic use at cost price.

Halfway down the west side of Victoria Street was Jenny Smith's general store. On the corner of Panmure Street and Kinloch Street was White's grocery shop, while on the corner of Brown Street and Smieton Street was a Mace grocery store. On Kinloch Street, between Burnside Street and Brown Street was Miss Penny's general store, and Jimmy Carnie's shop was on the corner of Kinloch Street and Golf Street. All the above are now residential properties. Also, a small general store was operated by a Miss Perry, and was located at the corner of Norries Road and Mariner Street, Westhaven. Later, Archie Marshall's wife ran a craft and gift shop there.

In Ireland Street, at the foot of Carlogie Road at the end of the lane to the "Smokey Brig," was a flesher's shop and later a chip shop. In 2024 it is a domestic garage. At No.11 Ireland Street was a shop with a small window where Charlie Petrie made and sold his high quality pewter, silver, and stainless steel decorative arts and crafts items. Later it was Wilson's bicycle shop. Hugh Duncan then sold fruit and vegetables in that shop. (Note: all were south of Church Street.)

At the corner of Ireland Street and Station Road was Mr Irvine's gents' high-quality tailoring and outfitters shop. It was a time capsule, and his "dated" styles went out of fashion by the end of the 1950s. The dapper Mr Irvine walked to and from his shop, religiously wearing his striped trousers, morning coat, bowler hat, and umbrella. It was later a shoe shop followed by Mr Russell Winter, who ran a chiropody practice there.

At the foot of Station Road on the west side was the Bookstall, which closed at the end of the 1950s. In time, the building disappeared, and today a stone wall marks the spot. Dave Fyffe's garage was at No.19–21 Church Street, and next door at No.17 was Esther Fyffe's fruit and veg shop. It became a cobbler's shop, and later a shop used by Billy Fyffe's wife to sell pottery items.

Other small shops were located away from the main Streets. On the south side of Tennis Road at No.9 and 9A, where today stands two modern bungalows, was a Co-op grocery store and—later—Selwood's joinery premises. Beyond Clayholes at Bell's Farm is a fruit and veg shop. On the corner of Miller Street and Queen Street was Willie Spalding's (formerly manager of Bradburn's) grocery shop, followed by Cromar's grocery shop, which later became a hairdressing salon. At the foot of Fox Street (No.21A) was Bill Ferrier's electrical shop. In 2024, it is a joinery store/workshop run by Christie's. In Park Avenue at Nos.1–3 in the 1940s was a small photographic studio run by Astbury's. Later it was Iain McDougall's first hairdressing shop then became the Fobel Shop (ironmongers/picture framing) run by Alistair Thom. Today it remains an ironmongery Fobel Shop. At the corner of Philip Street and Queen Street was a sweetie shop—details otherwise not known.

At No.19 Station Road was Betty Ness's shop, selling delicious homemade tablet and toffees. Once attached to the north side of the gable end of this private property block was a long narrow wooden office at what was likely No.23. This was the base of a taxi operator, who in the 1950s ran a fleet of several large black taxis. That business was sold to a school friend of mine—John Robb (son of the Gas works manager)—who ran it for a short period. Moving to the north end of Station Road on the corner with Church Street was originally, in the late 1880s, a high-class grocery and wine and spirit business run by a Mr Dick. The company was subsequently acquired by Bradburns, who also ran a country delivery service. Willie Spalding managed this shop, assisted by Alan Ferguson. Upstairs is the Panmure Snooker Club premises, established in 1912 and still in existence today.

Along the west side of Station Road was the high wall of the coal yard (some remnants still seen as part of the Co-op's premises), and this wall continued around the corner into High Street where, incorporated into the wall, were the offices of coal merchants Thomas Muir, Son and Paton, and Smith Hood and Son.

Station Road to Ferrier Street South Side

In 2024, the wall in the High Street has been replaced by a parade of small retail units, i.e, Franco's Café, the Nickel and Dime hardware store, and a Pet Care shop. Prior to this were Alan Fenton's shoe shop, Up and Coming school wear, the Bank of Scotland, Finn &Co. hairdressers, Nichol's Bikes, and Portrait Photos.

Beyond the shops is the entrance to the Co-op supermarket, and on the west side of Lochty Burn was Ritchie Harper's hairdressing business at No.5 (later

Carnoustie Chippie) and, at No.7, Jack Black's butcher shop which later became George's Chinese Take Away and is now a takeaway called Hung Wan.

Further east, roughly where the library is now located, was Mr Moonie's sweet shop with two steps up to the front door. Mr Moonie was a regular all-year-round sea swimmer, and was the man who taught me, my brother Peem, and Billy Coffin to swim at Arbroath Baths on Thursday evenings. On the corner of Fox Street and No.31 High Street is Connelly Yeoman estate agents—previously a Co-op grocery shop, McKerchers Insurance, and an art gallery.

Immediately past the disused Strachan's Art Deco garage is, at No.41, a gift shop called HayM. Previously, a gift shop called Links to Scotland and a café, a music shop called Reel to Reel, and—in the 1960s—a labour exchange. On the corner of Bonella Street at No.49 High Street is Sweets and Treats. In the 1950s–60s, this was Harry McKay's grocers and wine and spirit store. Later it was Olive's (second) Flower Shop, and then a bicycle shop run by George Duncan, following which is was a Christmas Elves shop.

At No.51 High Street is a takeaway, King Khan, which was previously Fred's Chipper. Then, at No.53 is Beau Boutique—previously Tiny Tots clothing, owned and run by Mrs Stark and her daughter. Previously the business housed Stevensons, then Soutars (the butcher). Pixie Stix, a fine goods and novelty shop, is situated at No.55 and was previously the TSB bank. At No.57 is Findlay's Hairdresser, which was previously Goodfellows bakery shop. At No.63 is the Banking Hub—previously J. Myles solicitor, an estate agent, and Joe Duncan's wholesale shoe shop. Koli's grilled chicken and burger shop is at No.69; prior to this, it was a cycle shop, then Holland's Pet Shop, and later Ally Donaldson's Pet Shop.

The Sun Lounge is at No.71, which was previously McDiarmid's Jewellers, and—before that—'Sonny' Duncan's wholesale carpet shop. It was then Robb's Sweetie Shop. Inner Balance is at No.75. On the corner of Park Avenue is an empty shop. Recently it was McLelland and Burney Opticians, but in

A view of Carnoustie High Street, taken from the roof of De Marco's Café at the top of Park Avenue. At the bottom right of the photo—by chance—is my mum with my wee sister Jean in a pram. She is chatting to someone while Peem patiently waits next to them.

the 1950s–1970s it was Landsburgh's high-class grocery store, managed by Graham Landsburgh.

Continuing along the south side of the High Street is the Premier Foods Store. In the early 1900s up to around 1970s, this was De Marco's ice cream parlour, run by Ada and Beth de Marco, which featured an outside terrace. It was Italian-owned, and boasted quality marble flooring and green cane chairs. To my lasting horror, this unique building was demolished in the 1970s, and Johnstone Stores took over the new premises which was opened by Ernie Wise of Morecambe and Wise fame. Later, Graham Landsburgh took over the store and ran it under the Spar symbol.

Moving along to No.89 High Street is the Our Carnoustie charity shop. In the early 1900s up to around late 1950s this shop was a branch of Scotland's largest chain of shops, trading as the Buttercup Dairy with its distinctive tiled doorway. Next door today, at No.93, is the SNP office, which was previously the Carnoustie Co-op Chemist shop once managed by Margaret Sturrock (nee Kennedy) of Scryne and by Mrs Mollan. It was also Martine's hairdressing shop. Next door was the Royal Bank of Scotland, and on the west side of that building were the offices of Caesar and Young solicitors.

In the gap between the next building is the entrance to the Dibble Theatre. This building was originally David McLagan's joinery workshop. He was a prominent football player for Carnoustie Panmure, who suffered a serious road crash resulting in a metal plate being fitted behind his forehead. Beyond the theatre are the rooms of the Baptist Church, which were originally the Co-op's ladies' outfitters shop, the shoe shop, and the gent's outfitters at No.105. Mr Herd (father of Morag) of Westhaven was manager of this department. The town's public library was at No.107. At the corner of Ferrier Street and High Street was Findlay, then Blackwood's butchery shop—now an Indian takeaway shop called New Golden Wok.

The Co-op's butchery shop was at the top west side of Ferrier Street, now housing. This marks the commencement of Dundee Street. Scotbet bookmakers' shop is at Nos.1–3 Dundee Street. At the time of writing, this business is about to cease trading here and is to move to No.100 High Street north side. At No.25 Dundee Street was John Yool's grocer's shop. This store was later to be Ferris the chemist shop. Next door, at No.27, was Anderson's drapery and haberdashery shop—now a café named Gather which incorporates Nos. 25 and 27.

At this point we cross the road to walk back along the north side of Dundee Street. At No. 52 is J.B. Sexton plumbers. This was, for over 30 years from the 1950s, the ironmongery shop of the legendary Mr Pat Birse—a Town Councillor. At No.50 is the Imperial takeaway. This was previously The Pepperbox. The Booze Store is at Nos. 34 and 36; this was previously Norman Donaldson's (Young's) newsagents, and also L.K. Dobson's TV shop. Mary Dunbar (previously Johnston store's manager) ran a clothes and crockery shop here, and Joan Woodford had a flower and veg shop in the same premises. Next door, at No.32, is Hair Design—previously a fruit and veg shop, it was Olive's first flower shop.

At No.6, Cunningham the chemist—later Tom Mackie Chemist and Douglas Kydd chemist—was situated, and is now a veterinary practice. Wm Low & Co. had two windows at No.4, and Keiller's Bakery—with one window—was next door at No.2. Those two shops are now, today, Boots the chemist shop. The Keiller's shop was Carnoustie's second Post Office prior to the Queen Street office. Before becoming part of Boots, Keiller's was Strachan's laundrette.

At No.124 High Street is Indo Spice. Previously this was D.T. Wilson's store, and later Scottish Gas services, then Scotland & Dawson. Dave McNicol's golf shop is at No.122. In the 1950s, this was Henderson's Emporium, with a side window up the passage to the back door of J.M. Bakery. Later, it was D.T. Wilson's. J.M. Bakery is at No.118, previously Alan Craigie's bakery which had run from the early 1950s through to around 1980. My close pal was young Alan, son of the owner. Sadly, Alan Jr. was excited more by micro-electronics than baking and selling pies, and to the great disappointment of his father he didn't enter the flourishing business. There is some word that Cunningham had operated a bakery there prior to Craigie's.

At No.114 is Blake's charity shop. Previously, this was McKay & Stewart the plumbers, and later Stormont's plumbers, but long before that—in the mid-19th Century—was Carnoustie's first Post Office. The double-fronted window next door at No.112 is The Haven charity shop. In the 1950s, this was Peebles grocery shop—part of a Dundee-based company. Miss Fyffe was the manager. Later, it became Watt's electrical shop, then Clydesdale's TV/electrical shop, following which it was to be occupied by the Victoria Wine company.

On the corner of High Street and Queen Street was No.108: Nicolls, the biggest and busiest bakery shop in the town, owned and run by Ken Hutcheson. D.T. Wilson's operated there, and then it became a sports shop. Today it is operated by A&G Properties. Nicoll's also ran the ballroom and tea rooms upstairs, with entry at No.2 Queen Street. It may also have been D.T. Wilson's furniture shop for a time.

Crossing Queen Street, we come to Sturrock's computer shop at No.106, which was previously Paterson's shoe shop—managed by Mrs Adam. She was the mother of Helen Adam (the well-known local figure who contracted polio at 18 years old. Helen taught English and history, and reached her 90th birthday). Later it was George Robertson's jewellery shop, and then Peter McLean's jewellery shop. Mr Robertson did the make-up for Newton Panbride Drama Group. The building was later home to Cargill hairdressers.

At No. 106 is the barber's shop, while at No.104 is Titanic Pizza shop; this was once High's fish shop. Located at No.102 is a hairdresser, while at No 100 was the old McDougall's (previously High's) fish shop, managed by Mr and Mrs Kirkcaldy; it later became the Tea Cosy café. At the time of writing, it is about to be occupied by Scotbet bookmakers. EFES fast food takeaway is at No.98. Previously, in the 1950s–60s, Stevenson's dry cleaners were situated here, managed by Nan Ramsay (nee Hunter).

McDougall's newsagent shop is at No.96; this was previously part of the YMCA and Wm Low shop, prior to moving to where the Co-op is today. At No.84 is Olive's flower shop. (Olive had previously run two flower shops in the town, and this was the top flower shop of its day.) Sadly she died prematurely, and the business name continues under new ownership. The west part of Olive's shop was for several years in the 1950s Johnstone's Stores grocery shop. No.80 is Visions T-shirts and hoodies—previously Simpson's bookshop and McArthur's chemist. Ewart's butcher shop is at No.72, previously Nelson Miller's butchers with Bert Scott in charge. In the 1950s, Bert won £75,000 on the football pools. Belle's cards and gifts shop is at No.70; this was previously Hazel Lambert's sweet shop, and also Inner Balance.

Gents' hairdresser Guys and Cutz is at No.68 This was once Soutar's radio &TV shop. No.60 is currently an empty shop. This was previously the Bottom Drawer café, also selling Scoop 'n' Save cereals. The company was run by Marjorie and Murray Ramsay for 30 years; Murray also sold and fitted blinds. Whittaker's optician is at No.58. That store was previously Mrs Anderson's haberdashery, and Norman Huscroft and his wife ran a grocery shop in the 1960s which was previously a clothing shop. At No.54 today is the Harbour Gallery, run by Bill Johns. This was previously "Woodies" (Mr Wood's) tiny newspaper shop, which was a mega-store for fireworks in the 1950s and 60s.

At No.44 was Christie's newspaper shop, which later became McLagan's and, in 2022–23, was a charity shop with a 'warm space' during huge rises in heating costs for some. Monkey Makes is a crafts/curiosity shop at No.32, previously Gold Stitch and a barber. It was also Jones' tobacconist, Express Cleaners, and the Brother knitting machine and wool shop. Nu-me is a ladies' hairdressers at No.30. Previously the unit was home to Pre-Amado and a children's shoe shop. Before that, it was Bob Pirie's fruit shop and Jones' tobacco shop.

Café Simpson's is at No.28. This was, back in the 1950s, Margaret McLean's ladies' outfitters. (Note: The shops and flats above were built by a Miss Paris in the late 19th century; hence the name "Paris Place.") At No.24 is Walker & Dunnet. This was a shop owned or run by the town council. In post-WW2 years it was a place to dispense dried milk, cod liver oil, and orange juice. In the 1950s it was the Carnoustie Publicity and Development offices, run by Mr Bill Cumming. On the west side of the lane, beside Dr McConnell's rest garden (now flats), was Ethel Grieve's fruit and veg shop, and later a fish shop. To the west of that was Swan's (Swannie's), a long-time favourite café and jukebox place. (Hot orange drinks were a favourite in the 1950s.) Later, this became a bike shop and then a dry cleaner's shop.

We now take a look at Queen Street, starting on the east side. Mr and Mrs Gowan's small grocery shop (next door to the Post Office) was located at No.7 Queen Street. Later, Mr and Mrs Hughes also ran a grocery shop there for several years. After that, a cafe called Crumbs operated, and in 2024 that small shop became a Thai restaurant. Across the road at No.8 is the Granary, and at No.6 and No.6A is J.E.H.L. Beauty. Previously this was Lister's flower shop. At Nos.3 and 4 is Quirky, selling keepsake gifts. This was Willie Clark's bicycle shop. He was otherwise known as "Spuggie," and had a small fishing boat at Westhaven. At No.2 was the stairway to Nicholl's tearoom and dance hall.

Links Avenue to Corner Hotel South Side

In Links Avenue was Leon Buller's shoe repair shop (with a glorious glowing red fire in the grate). The sweet shop, opposite where Moir's chip shop was (beside the very large tree seen in photos), was run by Fred Bisset and later Bobby Carr's Barber Shop. Mr and Mrs Wallace, who lived in Shamrock Street, ran a fruit and veg shop at No.51. Next door, at No.53, Harry Sutton ran a newsagent shop

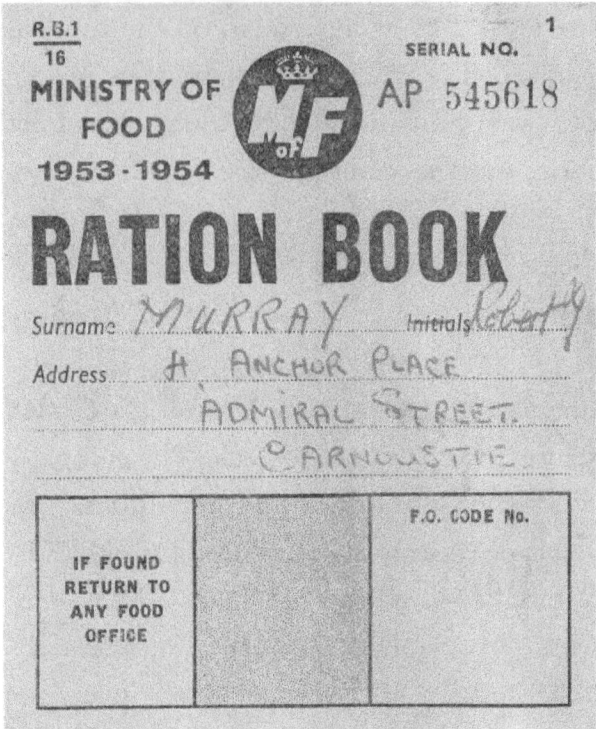

My ration book of 1953–54. Inside was a record of products bought by mum, i.e. meat (from Nelson Millar) and eggs, fat, cheese, bacon, and sugar from the Co-op.

previously operated by Miss Thoms. No.53 is at the top of Mayfield Lane (a.k.a. "Fishy Lane"). Peter D'Annunzio also had a shoe repair shop in the lane.

At No.65 was Findlay's bakers—now a hairdresser's shop called House of Handsome. At No.71 (opposite what was Alex Reid's garage and petrol station) was the Co-op West End Grocery store. And at No.73 was L.K. Dobson's radio and TV shop, where TV rentals were hired out. This is now Selwood's undertaker's offices and service room. At the corner of Burnside Street and Dundee Street was Smith's chip shop. Beyond this is now Brunton's architects offices, which was once an ironmongers business.

At Nos.91 and 101 Dundee Street were shops which are now dwellings. One was run by Barney Froggart, who sold fish.

Links Avenue to Corner Hotel North Side

At Nos.88–90 is Miller's furniture and carpet shop, previously the Regal Cinema. Prior to the lane was St Anne's RC Church, and at No.112 was a Co-op dry cleaner's shop—now a house. At No.118 was the Labour Hall (the USDAW and other unions met here), and at No.122 was a bookmakers office which is now Authentic Counselling. On the Corner of West Path and Dundee Street, at No.132, was Ronnie Lawson's sweet shop. In the 1950s, Jimmy Tate opened a new building and ran a barber's shop at No.132 (now a charity shop)

and a wool/knitwear shop at No.134 which is today Strachan's Care Services.

At No.158 was Norrie's fruit and vegetable shop. Moving further along, at No.166 Dundee Street in the 1980s–'90s David Black ran a butcher's shop, while during the 1950s, 60s and 70s Mr Boyle ran the Post Office at No.168.

Corner Hotel to James Street South Side

Today, a Co-op self-service shop is located near the Corner Hotel on Barry Road. This is on the site of a petrol station (Esso and Burmah) which operated there in the 1990s. At No.31 Mrs Davidson ran a grocery shop. This is now a private dwelling. Another grocery shop was located on Barry Road on the corner with Victoria Street. It was a double-fronted (two windows) property, run by the Dickson family. Nowadays this is an enlarged property which accommodates a Spar grocery business previously run by Graham Landsburgh for several years, which is now owned by C.J. Lang Wholesale Grocers of Dundee. A hundred yards along the pavement from that Spar store is a property/financial planning office which was, when I lived in Barry Road in the 1940s, run as a shop called Warren's.

Corner Hotel to James Street North Side

Based at No.6 is a Premier Convenience store (previously a V.G. Foodstore). McFarlane's newsagent was at No.8 and is now the Steeple chip shop. In earlier times, this was "Tattie Thamson's" potato office.

Over the years, directories of businesses in the town have been prepared and published. Dundee and Arbroath directories are freely available online. The above is merely an attempt to log those shops operating at the time of writing, with a little background information.

Doctors' Surgeries

Doctors' surgeries took up spaces on the main shopping area. On the east corner of Bonella Street and High Street was Dr P.D.C. McKay's surgery, and the property at the furthest west end of the terrace of villas (west of the road leading to Balfour Place) was Dr McConnell's surgery.

"A chapter likely to create some arguments about who traded when and where!"

Some Favourite Shops

"Retailing revolutions have seriously changed the town!"

As I grew up in the town in the 1950s, when there was a population of around 3,000 people (in 2025 it is around 12,000), there was a self-sufficient industrial and commercial economy in the Burgh. Post-war full employment in the jute works, the foundry, the shoe factory, the vitriol/agricultural plant, and the jam factory, was enjoyed by the local population. Alongside this went a lively independent retail sector, with a wide range of shops covering every facet of retailing.

I have tried to describe elsewhere the general shopping scene, but in this section I'd like to pick out a few of my favourite shops. First, I must remind readers this was a time prior to self-service stores. Each shop had its own "well-kent" owners who were local characters.

Betty Ness's toffee and tablet shop in Station Road was a must while out for a Sunday afternoon family walk. Her range of delicacies was literally mouth-watering. Also, on Station Road (on the corner with Ireland Street) was the time capsule of Mr Irvine's gents' tailoring business. I was not of an age to buy from him, and his upmarket clothing was out of my father's price range. But Mr Irvine was still to be seen walking to and from his shop, dressed immaculately in his morning suit, striped trousers, and smart jacket or coat, complete with bowler hat and brolly. Quite definitely a figure unchanged from Edwardian days.

Ethel Grieve's fruit and vegetable shop—now gone and replaced by flats next to the lane beside the Lochty Burn and adjacent to Dr McConnell's Rose Garden—was also a favourite. Her fresh fruit and vegetables were strikingly aromatic. High's fish shop was an interesting shop to visit. I always admired how Mr and Mrs Kirkcaldy could, without gloves, possibly gut and fillet fish on freezing cold days. (Their son, Drew Kirkcaldy, became a senior footballer). John Yool ran his own private grocer's store (underneath the block of flats situated above the shops opposite the lane leading to Terrace Road) single-handedly. He had an unhurried pace of his own, which was at odds with my hectic hustle and bustle employment in Wm Low's (now Boots the Chemist). Anderson Drapers was located next door to John Yool.

Pat Birse, who ran an ironmongery shop (next to the grass area immediately east of Carnoustie Parish Church), was a character with a likeable high profile. He was a Burgh Councillor, and a man with a wild and cheeky sense of mischievous fun. He was once reputed to have driven his car onto the Championship golf course over a walk bridge, but the next day nobody—including Pat—could find a way to drive it off the course. It remains a mystery to this day!

Carnoustie was fortunate in that every type of retail shop was represented in the town. When large supermarkets were developed, all the "independent" retail sectors were contained under one roof—fish, butchery, fruit and vegetables, delicatessen, and even dry cleaning—resulting in the gradual disappearance of so many small, specialist shops. In 2025, the Co-op in the High Street alongside the Lochty Burn offers a small supermarket (previously run by Wm Low & Co.), but the nearest large supermarkets—Morrisons, Tesco and Asda—are based in Arbroath, and offer a wider range of produce. Such a shame for the town, but it is all determined by what is known as "footfall"—or, in Carnoustie's case, a lack of it.

As mentioned earlier, in the 1950s a small double-fronted shop on the corner of Victoria Street and Barry Road offered groceries from a shop operated by the Dickson family. Later, it was developed by Landsburgh's into a more spacious Spar grocery mini-market, and still today it is a Spar store—now owned by C.J. Lang, a wholesale grocers from Dundee who supply the stock and merchandising aids. One other favourite was DeMarco's ice cream parlour/tearoom on the corner of Park Avenue and High Street. To everyone's horror in the 1970s, the majestic ornate building with classic Italian-style marble flooring—complete with patio—was recklessly demolished. In its place was built a large self-service grocery store operated by Johnstone's Stores, and later by Landsburgh's. in 2025 it is a Premier store, open for extended hours seven days a week and selling wines/spirits and groceries.

The greatest sadness is that the town, from the earliest years, has lost numerous shops and the hard-working people who ran them. In 2025, grocery shopping is limited to the aforementioned large Co-op store, a Premier store and a Spar shop at Barry Road, resulting in many empty shops and some financial or insurance offices. A retail marketing expert sums up Carnoustie's shopping demise thus: "The advent of the supermarket, almost at a stroke, spelt the end of specialist shops. This has been more seriously compounded by online shopping. It doesn't help, but Carnoustie is not alone with this problem. Someday, deliveries will be made by drone, thus wiping out most retail units."

"Step forward the local services of plumbers, electricians and joiners!"

Telegraph messages were sent by wire from one Post Office to another. The message was printed in strips, which were then attached to an appropriate paper card, e.g. Weddings, Deaths, or Congratulations. This was a speedy way to send an important or urgent message. A "telegram boy" or "telegraph boy" on a motor bike would then deliver the message. I was never aware of a telegram girl.

The Post Office

Although not necessarily described as a shop, I always found visits to the Post Office particularly interesting. Whether I was dealing with something associated with my work or depositing my saved message boy "tips," the smell of ink, glue, or the rubber date stamps—and the general buzz—caught my imagination and suggested a hectic, essential national service.

Carnoustie's first Post Office was in what, today, is Blake's charity shop at No.128, followed by premises at No.2 Dundee Street which later became Keiller's bakery shop and eventually part of what is now Boots the Chemist shop. The town's third Post Office was located at Queen Street. The original building—consisting of the counter and sales area and the sorting office—still exists, with the latter now residential properties. My experiences in the Post Office centred around buying stamps and postal orders, but telegrams were another popular service provided. In the 1950s and '60s, "the telegram boy" rode around town on a small motorbike delivering telegrams with news of deaths, births, or urgent business notices. Telegrams also featured at wedding celebrations, with "best men" given the welcome and sometimes humorous task of reading out congratulatory messages to the bride and groom.

Bill Wallace lived next door to us at No.6 Shamrock Street, and I recall he darted about the town as the town's only telegram boy. Bill ultimately became a Post Office manager at Kirriemuir.

Picture Houses

"Sixpenny bench seats at the front!"

Carnoustie boasted two cinemas: The Pavilion, now replaced by a block of flats on the east side of Park Avenue (the road leading towards the sea from The Cross), and The Regal on Dundee Street (across the road from the Kinloch Care Centre) which, as of 2025, is the showroom for Miller's furniture and carpets business.

The Pavilion was built originally as a Playhouse, to accommodate the entertainers who originally had put on *al fresco* shows on the seafront. The Regal had no stage, and had previously been a church. It was well-run, and the staff in the 1950s was mainly the Buist family and Stan. They kept the place clean and warm, and I can still smell the combination of bleach (or Harpic) along with the more pleasantly-perfumed lavender sprays. When the cinema closed, the building became a sports and social club with a bar, and later a carpet and furniture store for Millers.

When we—the rowdy lot on the 6d (2.5p) front-row benches—stamped our feet and screamed at hair-raising (or not!) tense moments or stirring images on the silvery screen, Stan would rush down the aisle and bark "Quiet!" and shine his dazzling torch all over us. Seat prices in both cinemas were arranged as follows: front row bench, 6d (2.5p), next two or three rows of proper seats, 9d. All other seats downstairs 1/3d or nearer the back 2/- (10p). Upstairs was 2/3d. While it was a cinema, a small shoe factory was operated at the rear. When that closed, the

Hollywood on the stage had come to Carnoustie! The two "leading lights" in those exceptional shows were Ian Spalding and Alma Donald. My own experience there was to play the part of the Sheriff in *Finian's Rainbow*.

British Legion moved in from premises in Kinloch Street, opposite the 19th Hole.

The Pavilion cinema was built in 1912, originally as the town's concert hall to accommodate theatrical stage productions. Later, it was occasionally used to present excellent productions by Carnoustie Musical Society for a week, annually, for top Hollywood musicals such as *South Pacific*. The annual productions were so popular that, on the evenings of the show, cars and buses lined the length of the High Street and Dundee Street—with a policeman on points duty at The Cross!

The cinema was also booked most years for a three-evening, "three act" play performance by Newton Panbride Dramatic Club. No policeman at the Cross was required this time, but the plays always obtained high praise from local newspaper reporter Harry Chapman. Parts I was able to (or tried to) play were Hopcroft Minor in *The Happiest Days of your Life* and Carnoustie Bly in *Sailor Beware*. In the 1950s, both cinemas featured midweek serials—for example *Flash Gordon*, *Spider-Man* and *Superman*. By picking different evenings, we could go to both cinemas and follow the serials.

"Quite a thrill to appear on the big stage!" (Show off!)

Public Houses

"Come away boys—it's 9.30 now, you know!"

There are so many factors in the life and success of any town, and Carnoustie is no different. In the 1950s it boasted what one may call a balanced society, encompassing its industries, retail, and commerce, and the consequential mix of residential properties both private and public. Carnoustie was a self-supporting town.

With a healthy mix of clubs and societies reflecting hobbies, youth, sport, music, and drama, there seemed to be no shortage of ways in which people could occupy their free time. The town even boasted a skating pond. Yes, there were numerous ways in which people of all ages could engage in entertainment and activities with a balanced lifestyle. Public houses, the "local" pub, provided for many an aspect of freedom, good company, and recreation. And this being a "lang toon" necessitated several pubs.

When my friend Willie Yool came home on leave from the Royal Navy, I heard from him the stories of the great supply of "Blue liners" he enjoyed. These were cigarettes made especially for naval personnel, and sported a thin blue line along each cigarette. I heard also about his free daily tot of rum, which he enjoyed. A tot was certainly more than a "nip"—"Almost like a glassful," he explained. Willie missed his tot and, at 18 years of age, felt the need for some alcoholic refreshment. He encouraged me to join him in the 19th Hole pub in Ferrier Street. Thus, at the "under-age" of 17, I joined him for a pint. That was my first and only ever under-age drink. I didn't enjoy it, and queried why there was a piece of mouse dirt in my drink—only to be advised it was a hop. Much to the amusement of Willie, by then a regular daily drinker, I didn't finish my drink and in fact never drank a pint again.

Pubs (public houses) in Carnoustie in the 1950s were The Station, The Kinloch Arms, The Golf Inn, The 19th Hole, and The Stag. It's notable that the above are still functioning in 2024. In addition, some hotels in the 1950s also offered "drink" at a public bar — such as Carlogie House, Earlston, Panmurebank, Brax, Morven, Glencoe, and the Bruce Hotel and Aboukir. (The Dalhousie Hotel was a temperance hotel.) It's true to say that the town was well-endowed with "drinking" spots. Of course, running alongside the same timeline as pubs, golf club also offered bar facilities—including Carnoustie Golf Club, New Taymouth, Caledonian, Dalhousie and Mercantile. In more recent times, a Links Bar operated in Dundee Street, and the West End Bar (now the Craw's Nest) on Barry Road.

Reflecting changes in social attitudes, legal opening hours for pubs have changed. In the 1950s, the hours were 11 am until 2.30 pm, followed by 5 pm until 9.30 pm. Gradually, the hours were extended to 10 pm. In 2024, hours vary according to publicans' decisions, and can be from 10 am until midnight.

One rule in the years up to the 1950ss was that pubs closed on Sundays—unless you were a "bona fide traveller" and came from at least three miles away from the pub. Some clever customers overcame this rule by travelling by bus from, for example, Monifieth to Carnoustie to enjoy a Sunday "dram," or vice-versa. This law was scrapped in the 1960s.

"Yes, Carnoustie's pubs have survived!"

Dancing "Hot Spots"

"'Slow, slow, quick-quick, slow!' to Dave Torrie and his band!"

The very popular Saturday evening dance venue during my teenage years was the Y.M.C.A. (Young Men's Christian Association) Hall, otherwise known as the "Y.M." This was the building on the north side of the High Street immediately west of Olive's flower shop (in 2024), and today is marked as No.84 High Street.

In my earlier, timid days, I had a Saturday evening routine. Our plan was to go to the first house of the "pictures" at the Pavilion or Regal. (Both cinemas operated a "first" house which ran from 6 pm until around 8.30 pm, and a "second" house running from around 8.30 pm until about 10.45 pm. Each "house" presented a "B"-film, then Pathé News followed by the main "A" film. On emerging from the cinema at the end of the "first house" there was always a long queue, sometimes in wind or rain, for the "second" house.) Then, at 9 pm, we'd buy a quarter pound of toffee sweeties at "Swannie's" café, then pay nine pence (3p in new money) to watch the dancing from the balcony in the Y.M.). Eventually, we picked up courage to dance on the spacious dance floor and pay two shillings for the privilege. The regular entertainer was Dave Torrie with his fiddle, drums and accordion band—Bothy Nicht music! But there were hazards. Yes, in the late 1950s on Saturday evenings the Dundee "teddy-boys" frequented the Y.M. and brought with them some tough "fighting" characters. We decided to steer clear.

During the summer months, the undoubted attraction was the Friday evening teenagers' dances in the Beach Hall. This was a must—the large hall was usually packed. The dances ranged from slow (very slow) foxtrots, quicksteps, and jiving, including at least one or two essential "ladies' choices"—with lights turned down low and the rotating crystal ball gleaming in multi-colours, giving the ballroom a warm, romantic feel. Those regular dances were occasionally supplemented by "one-offs," held in church halls. I can remember, probably around 1956 or 1957, a dance arranged in Barry West Church Hall, on the spot at the west corner at the junction of the main Barry Road and the road to Barry Mill. Another venue for "one-offs" was the Episcopalian Church Hall in Holyrood Street.

Whatever the venue we attended, there was always the distinctive welcoming smell of "Slipperene"— a dusty spray that was applied to the dance floor which, I imagined, was to aid the "glide." Added to that, of course, was the mix of girls' perfume. All of it created that captivating teenager atmosphere.

"Ah, those were the days!"

Favourite Walks around the Town

"Carnoustie is central for so many favourite walks!"

Despite changes caused by the railway and additional roads, the variety of local walks around Carnoustie will not have changed much over the past 200 years. The 'lang' town lends itself to several circular walking routes—namely, to:

Barry

From The Cross to Barry Village, then take the first right after crossing the road bridge to Barry Mill. Thereafter, at the Mill follow the path over the narrow bridge (which was the ancient route linking Barry to Panbride) to the area of Shanwell cemetery and on to Lovers' Lane, emerging at the top of West. Then along Terrace Road back to the Cross.

Westhaven

From the centre of the town, walk to the sea front then eastwards to Westhaven, followed by crossing the "Steeny Brig." Then walking up Westhaven Farm Road (to the old Panbride parish church), and then along behind Carnoustie House grounds and down West Path.

Craigmill Den

From the top of Queen Street (on old maps referred to as East Path), take the route to Panbride Parish Church and follow the road to Craigmill Den (with the option of taking a stroll which starts at the Loupin' Stane beside the cottages at the entrance to the graveyard, then on to the Fairy Steps). Once down the hill to Craigmill Den, follow the track alongside the burn to the Bleachfield, then walk back into town along Arbroath Road. This walk may be greatly extended by not following the burn to the Bleachfield, but taking the road to Scryne then down the hill to Easthaven. From Easthaven, the return to Carnoustie can be made easily by following the cycle path route or walking along the shore. By doing the latter, you may be able to guess where George Maule, 3rd Earl of Panmure, may have created a harbour ("Mauleshaven"?) for ships to await the high tide for the sail to Dundee.

Monikie Monument

For the more adventurous, a walk from the centre of the town to "The Panmure Memorial Monument" may be of interest. After walking to the western end of Barry Road, at the roundabout, take the road northwards to Monikie, passing by Pitskelly and continuing up the long "Marches." Enter the wood on the left, opposite an entrance to the Panmure Estate on the east side of the road. Follow the route through the trees, and note Camus Cross—allegedly where the Danish invader is buried. After passing a modern dwelling on your left, you reach Monikie Monument. (Note: The 106-foot-high monument built in 1839 by the grateful tenants of the Earl of Panmure was in recognition of his generosity by not charging rents or back rents during the famine years of the 1870s. The urn at the top was added in memory of three estate servants who died in the Tay Rail Bridge disaster in 1879. Panmure House, the home of successive Earls, was built in 1664 and demolished in 1955.)

Town Walks

For the less ambitious, there are many variations of walks around the town. Take time to consider the location of numerous locations of cottages and terrace of cottages, some with long feus. These are amongst the oldest properties in the town, and were most likely the homes of "hand loom weavers"—some of which were, in the earliest days, built nearby to a well.

Barry/Buddon Army Grounds

Commencing at Barry Railway crossing, a walk to the nearby Memorial Garden commemorating Marines of 45 Commando, who gave their lives in the 1982 conflict in the Falklands, and then onwards to the lighthouses, returning to Barry Railway Station.

Westhaven

"Two plump rabbits, Mr Murray—there's half a crown to you!"

When our family moved from Annfield Cottages, Barry Road, Carnoustie, to Anchor Place, Admiral Street, Westhaven, my world was transformed. The rather restricted scope around my Barry Road cottage home was in sharp contrast to the new Westhaven world which beckoned.

We had enjoyed a spacious garden at Annfield which was home to a hen-run of bantam hens and two rabbit hutches, yet there was limited freedom to explore beyond the garden gate. With the curiosity streak of a four-year-old, I set off one day with a nearby playmate and found myself exploring the course of the Barry Burn. Engrossed as I was, I remember getting downstream as far as the bridge at the railway line and was having some fun when I heard a loud scream. It was my mum, and she was furious. She pulled down my pants and gave me a hard spank—much to the amusement of some workmen high up on a crane in the Anderson Grice foundry. In hindsight, I can now realise how concerned she must have been.

Several other memories during my years there are still clear to me. I recall the shared outside toilet, which was located about 30 yards from our front door. A battery torch was required on dark windy nights (or a lit candle on calm nights) to help pick my way to the toilet door—sometimes to discover, only by pushing the door, that the loo was occupied. On a cold or wet night, that was not pleasant. Once inside the toilet on gale-force evenings, there was only the noise of trees blowing and the door shaking on creaky hinges, to say nothing of the "sneck" threatening to unhitch itself at any moment.

A panic arose one evening, before we had gone to bed, when the paraffin heater in the house started emitting black smoke. I'm sure I learned later that the wick had started to burn, causing a thick cloudy atmosphere. Luckily, dad was off duty and was able to immediately deal with the panic.

Two scary memories of quiet evenings at home remain with me. Both were unsettling. One was quite close to us. As mum explained, "Don't worry; that's just the pitter patter of mice footsteps on the ceiling roof." The more scary and threatening moment was the distant distraction of the long, slow, low drone of German bombers high above us. Luckily, in hindsight, I now realise Carnoustie would not have been an enemy target, although on bombing run nights the Germans may have been hoping to target the Tay Rail Bridge or Barry Buddon Camp.

During the war years, food was scarce, and one day I was shocked to find the local butcher had appeared unexpectedly to take away the two rabbits which my brother and I had carefully tended as pets. Perhaps we hadn't looked after them as well as we had imagined, and dad had decided to "cash them in" for half a crown (2/6d or 12.5p). Perhaps the poor things were simply too old. It was a sad loss which taught me, at my young age, something about the war having a direct impact upon all of us.

Possibly the most disturbing event was when the long rake I was holding up on its end in the palm of my hand tipped off balance and came crashing down on my brother's head. By some amazing luck he was not hit by the "spike" side. I was in big trouble for my carelessness, and close to another bare-bottom spank!

Most memorable events were when an army pipe band happened to march along Barry Road just at the moment, we as a family, had walked from the cottage path to the roadside pavement. It was a stirring noise and when I imagine the trouble and worries of wartime it must have been an uplifting and gratifying moment for locals.

The transformation of our move to Westhaven hit me immediately. We were now "off the beaten track," and—even at a young age—I sensed the unique quiet world of 'the Ha'en' (That is, Westhaven). I became rapidly aware of the restricted world I must have had at Annfield. It took a tiny signal from one of the local children playing in the street to introduce the magic of Westhaven—it happened almost spontaneously. Feeling lost and timid to adventure out in my new world, I was gazing out of my upstairs bedroom window wishing I could be down there on the street playing with some boys and girls. After a while, one of the older looking girls—who was probably around ten or eleven years old—looked up, waved to me, and then beckoned me to join them. I must have looked a nervous soul in my new world, and I told mum who immediately said, "That's very nice of them—off you go and play with them!" My glorious world of Westhaven: in one moment, the seed of my exciting and unforgettable childhood days at "the Ha'en", was sown.

Thereafter, Peem and I met up with his close pal to be, Billy Coffin (whose father, we learned, came from Cornwall), and then the Scott family, the father of which was a Coastguard Officer. From that large family of girls, our pal Oliver (Ollie) was the only boy. Also living in the bespoke Coastguard terraced block of villas was our pal Douglas Keith, whose father was also a Coastguard Officer. I gained in confidence and, in addition to playing a variety of street games, I met up with Jim Ritchie. As he was two or three years older than me, I found myself helping him dig for bait and eventually fishing off the rocks with him. Later with Peem and Coffey, we found ourselves rowing out to sea, with Jim—our leader—who was charged with looking after fishermens' boats. The repeating annual seasons, and all that we experienced at every point in each year, was our joy. Westhaven, with all my friends, was a stable chapter in my early life.

"The Ha'en was my oyster, and the pearl was the harbour!"

Weather: Flooding, Snow and Gales

"Make sure he gets off at Barry School, please!"

Westhaven Beach, on the western edge of Carnoustie.

My first year at Barry school must have commenced in August 1945, when I was four years old and about to be five in October. We possibly moved to Admiral Street, Westhaven, in the later part of 1946 or early 1947. I have been able to calculate this, for I recall mum—rather than having me move to Carnoustie School in mid-term—arranged for me to continue attending Barry Primary School for the remainder of the 1945–46 session. This presented me with what was a nerve-wracking and testing experience.

Her solution was to walk with me from Admiral Street to the bus stop at Aboukir Hotel, and explain to the single-deck Bluebird Bus conductress that I was going to Barry School. This worked well—I paid my penny fare, and was prompted when to leave the bus. The return journey was not so relaxed. First, I had to safely look after my "return" penny bus fare all day and then make my way to the bus stop, luckily directly across the road from the school, to wait for the return bus. I had to make sure the bus driver saw me, then to explain my destination. This was followed by my anxious peering out of the sometimes-steamy window at landmarks along the route, then standing up—not too early or too late—ready to disembark. Mum was always waiting for me at the bus stop. In hindsight, I often wonder if those nervous days were when my sense of planning and responsibility started.

The unnerving journeys I had experienced to and from Westhaven, and the lonely walk to Barry School from Annfield Cottages, resulted in some personal doubts and worries. I should explain that the fields on the seaside of Barry Road and behind the school, and all around the Barry Burn, were often flooded in winter. This, I believe, was not only caused by severe rainfall but also exacerbated by high tides. Consequently, Barry Road itself was often under water all the way to school. My only route was to gingerly tip-toe along the top of the tufted grass verge. I became aware that in some parts where there was an entry to a field, the grass verge was non-existent. My feet were often wet, but—when there were gaps in the verge—jumping across spaces was liable to end in certain soaked legs or the fear of something worse! As has been mentioned, the fire guard around Miss Bell's glowing classroom fireplace was a regular spot for my wet shoes and socks.

During the harsh winter of 1947, there was a particularly serious snowstorm. By then we lived at Westhaven, and so the route home (before I had a bike and cycled home via the tunnel at Ferrier Street and along Tayside Street) was along the High Street. I clearly recall walking along the pavement with snow piled up well above my head.

Snowstorms and icy roads during my young days were met with conflicting feelings. Having a bicycle was a great advantage, as travel between home and school was simple and easy but deep snow or rutted frozen slushy roads were treacherous—as was black ice, when the roads looked wet but were in fact frozen and covered in lethal ice. Road maintenance in winter then was not so advanced, and icy ruts sometimes lasted for days. Excitement and joy were also in the air, however, with the arrival of snow and ice—especially if they appeared at weekends or holiday periods. Our favourite place to meet for sledging was the "Steeny Brig" (the railway bridge at Westhaven), which provided—when there was "good going"—a long run down to the top of the beach. On occasions when the "scaffie" truck came round to grit the roads, we were quick to run home to grab a brush and quickly take part in the anti-social act of brushing away the offending sand.

I think it was January 1953 when we experienced damaging gales across Scotland. While we were aware of rough seas and damage to some property and trees around Westhaven, the severity was brought home to me when, within days, we as a family made a visit to granny and granddad's croft at Dunninald. I suspect mum and dad made the journey for the sole reason to ascertain the level of fear and likely damage experienced by my mum's parents. Their sense of concern was confirmed. When we stepped off the "utility" Bluebird Bus, the scale of devastation was clear to see. The small but ancient plantation of beautiful tall beech trees some 400 yards away from granny's cottage had been flattened, and the magnificent grey-bark trees were lying in neat lines as if a giant had placed them there. On previous visits, we had become accustomed to climbing a small brick wall at the roadside then running freely through the grassy ground in the wood which was a haven for the most delicious ground-growing blue berries. That walk had always been a glorious experience, for we knew exactly where to find the sharp-flavoured berries. We were spoiled for choice with both wild raspberries and plump succulent soft gooseberries growing in the hedgerow. Sadly, our rich joys of nature were never the same after that gale. I look at that space nowadays and see how tall a "new wood" has naturally developed, and am able to state with some accuracy that it is now 71 years old.

Sadly, when we arrived at the Croft, granny and granddad's loss was immediately evident, for a similar beech tree plantation a mere 100 yards eastwards from their back door had also been felled. Unlike the first collection of trees, there was no grass and berries, for granddad had fenced off that entire wooded area as a hen-run. Their loss was clear to see, for the hen-houses had been flattened. I remember asking granddad what happened to the hens. "They're lying deid in the huts, or been blawn awa'. But the foxes will ha'e had a guid meal," he told me. His frank description put me off the idea of making a closer personal inspection.

As we travelled home that evening, I couldn't help thinking how someone—many years previously—had carefully and cleverly planned the small plantations, for they had spared the property from that damaging west wind.

"And as it happens, the new plantation survived the 2021 storm!"

Lost Buildings of Carnoustie

"Why did the Council have to throw away all that history, Robert?"

Streets and buildings—especially dwelling houses—in any settlement reflect history. At first glance, a visitor could question the odd mixture of properties throughout the town. Old cottages exist in almost every part of the town, except for properties on Carlogie Road and north of Church Street. In other parts of the town, such cottages and more modern substantial dwellings are found in an unplanned *ad hoc* fashion, and it is interesting to question why and where they had been built in such haphazard style. Was this to support early local industry? Cottages would pre-date other larger properties—were they part of the linen weaving industry, or simply there because a well was nearby?

Westhaven and Easthaven cottages would almost certainly have housed the fishing communities but, in the town, they seem interspersed in such an unplanned way alongside substantial dwellings of more recent times—except, of course, the many cottages built to a plan by James Smieton for his employees.

It is safe to say Carnoustie has few, if any, classical buildings. However, there are numerous examples of properties which reflect periods of time in the town's development. Examples are hotels such as Kinloch, Station, Dalhousie, Corner, and Aboukir, and of course Carnoustie House in its once-substantial grounds. Mr Smieton's Panmure Hall is a classic building of its time.

In the east end of the town, there are good examples of substantial stone-built Victorian villas—whether detached or semi-detached. It is Mr Kinloch who is regarded as the man that, in the early 19th Century, set about planning the streets and roads in the town.

And yet, it is interesting to note that Kinloch Street—the longest planned street in the town—displays the best example of the mix of properties built "cheek by jowl." Likewise, narrow streets leading off Queen Street also demonstrate the strange mixture of dwelling houses.

During my years in Carnoustie, I have seen several worthy buildings demolished. Best examples are the once-magnificent Panmure House (home to the Dalhousies), Carnoustie House, Dalhousie Golf Club, the Bandstand, and the iconic Wooden Golf starters box—all victims of "progress," with Panmure Hall having a last-minute reprieve in 2021. Of course, landmarks such as the Winter's shoe factory chimney and the gaswork tanks—although not "pretty"—have gone now too.

A family photo in 1950.
From L to R: Dad, Robbie, Isobel, James (Peem), Mum.

CHAPTER 4
Faith and Religion

Churches

"That's the kirk bell—run on, or you'll be late!"

For its size, the town of Carnoustie was well-served by a surprising number of churches. My family attended Barry Church when we lived in the village, and later when we lived at Annfield Cottage on Barry Road, Carnoustie. In fact, the Barry Church parish extends eastwards as far as West Path, Carnoustie. I can still recall at the appropriate moment leaving the service and, along with other children, going to Sunday School. On some occasions, we seemed to have to stand on the outside steps in the cold and rain until the teacher arrived.

When we moved to Westhaven in 1947, we attended Newton Panbride Church. The background to that church is that after the 1834 Disruption, the break-away Free Church of Panbride Parish—183 parishioners—worshipped in a barn, then a wooden shed, at Westhaven Farm. In 1854, the Earl of Dalhousie gave the congregation stone from his quarry to build a church on the Gallowlaw (once a hanging place). In 1929, it became known as Newton Panbride Church. A building on the south side of William Street was designated as a manse while the official manse was built.

In those days, each pew had a number at the end of the row and a brass frame into which a card was inserted, listing the names of the families allocated to that pew. In earlier days, payment was required to secure a space in the pew, but I think by 1947 there was a system of either putting money in the plate at the door

On good days, Mr Chambers held Bible Class meetings under the apple tree in the manse garden. From L to R:
Back row: James Murray (Peem), John Robb, Ronald Aitken, Harry Reid, Brian Wilson (?), Robbie Murray, Bill Fyffe.
Front row: Sylvia Chambers, [unknown], Lindsay Fleming, Aileen Rough, [unknown], Margaret Reid, Catherine Lawrence (?).

younger children—in our case "wee Jean," who was born in 1953. Our special lunch was usually steak pie, tatties, and dad's garden vegetables, followed by mum's special trifle. Dad had seven-eighths of a small bottle of stout, while Peem and I shared the remaining "wee drop" topped up with American cream soda. What a Sunday treat!

From Barry village, moving eastwards, the churches were located at Barry Bridge, the West Church—now demolished, with a small rest area in its place and a church hall located or by obtaining small envelopes into which my parishioners put their weekly offering, known as the Free Will Offering. We sat upstairs in a pew which, I think, was numbered 73. The church was almost packed each Sunday, and in our pew were two families—the Reids (usually Les, the dad, and Harry, Margaret and Angus) and the Murrays (dad, me, James (Peem) and Isobel). Some mums in those days probably remained at home to prepare Sunday lunch and look after

A happy day at our annual Sunday School picnic at Crombie Park.
From L to R: Robbie Murray, John Robb, Robert Seaton, At the back James Murray (Peem).

there too where I once attended a dance in 1957. Barry East Church was at the sharp bend in the road near the school. Congregations used to alternate between both churches. Before the R.C. Church in Thomas Street was built in the 1990s, the R.C. Church was situated at St Annes, Dundee Street—the building (now a private residence) was located opposite the Kinloch Care Home buildings.

All dressed up with neighbours in Admiral Street, Westhaven, for a Fancy Dress event at the church. James (Peem) Murray is front left and Robbie Murray is centre, both dressed as cowboys.

The Old Parish Church (technically with no parish) is in Dundee Street, opposite the car park at the top of Links Avenue. Funds to build the church were raised by events at the seafront, including bazaars. The cash ran out, and a steeple was never built. St Stephen's Church was also in Dundee Street, and opposite the short unnamed street which leads to Balfour Place. Mr Rettie, the builder/developer of Balfour Place, in the late 1890s requested a name for that short street, but it was never granted. When St Stephen's Church was demolished in the 1970/80s, Carnoustie's health centre occupied the space for several years prior to moving to Parkview Health Centre once it had been established at Barry Road. Blocks of flats now occupy the space. Today, a Baptist Church is located opposite the War Memorial and based in the previous property once occupied by the Co-op drapery and ladieswear shop.

Newton Panbride Church is located on Arbroath Road. Initially, the manse was a substantial private dwelling on the south side of William Street, pending the building of the manse we see today next door to the church. Built by the Dalhousie family, Panbride church has a long history. It served the parish including Muirdrum, Bleachfield, East Haven, and Scryne areas. The church houses a crypt in which Dalhousie family members are interred.

After great uncertainty due to the Church of Scotland's national re-assessment of needs, as I write this the plan is for Panbride Parish Church to be sold and Barry Church to be reduced to a community hall, while a union of the Barry, Carnoustie Parish and Newton Churches will be formed. The ancient artefacts in Panbride Church will be saved and stored in Newton Panbride Church.

A steady decline of church membership has taken place since the mid-1950s. Sadly, it seems to me the Church of Scotland delayed too long in finding ways to retain the interest of adults and to encourage young people to be part of the church.

My church involvement was an important part of my life!

Newton Panbride: Our Family Church

"Santa Claus has landed in the manse garden!"

Mum and dad were not deeply religious people, but from what I could gather they had both been brought up as regular church attenders—mum at Craig, near Montrose, and dad at Lunan Bay. I have a Bible at home with my father's mother's name written inside. Also, I do clearly remember mum telling me how she had to learn off by heart the "Shorter Catechisms." She evidently hated the prospect of having to memorise them then recite the text at Sunday school.

Mum's family were most definitely country people—her mother, Annie Hutcheson of the Esplin family, was born and brought up at Tigerton, near Little Brechin in the area of Balnamoon, deep in Angus farming lands. There are Esplins and Hutchesons buried in Menmuir Churchyard. Mum's father was born at Guthrie near Arbroath, and had

Newton Panbride Church Sunday School stage show in 1947. James (Peem) Murray is at front row extreme left, and Robbie Murray, shown wearing pyjamas, is 4th from right in the second row. Other names include: Ian Pate, Moira Pate, Harry Reid, Angus Reid and Margaret Reid, Billy Fyfe, David Grant, Billy Coffin, Aileen Lawrence and Catherine Lawrence, David Black, Irene Black, Jennifer Black, Jim Ritchie, Brian Winton, and Ronald Aitken.

you just need to read about Robert Burns' life.)

Life and work was "on the land," and I recall mum telling me that her mother had travelled by horse and cart to Brechin on market days to sell eggs. Mum was born at Boddin near Usan, Montrose, where her father had become farm manager and she walked three miles to school and church at Craig.

By modest contrast, my father's parents had a slightly different station in life. My grandmother was one of a local Edwards family which ran a nearby smiddy (blacksmith) business situated on the main Arbroath/Montrose Road, near Lunan village. They seemed to have had a financially rewarding connection in the farm engineering aspects of life back then. Strangely, that granny also had an illegitimate

moved to the Brechin area. My mother's mother had an illegitimate child before her marriage to my grandfather, George Taylor. (It was not uncommon in those days for men to marry ladies with an illegitimate child—

child before marriage to my grandfather, James Murray, who was one of three out-of-wedlock sons of Jane Murray. My father's father started his working life on farms, but it seems that some influence guided him to seek a different scope in life, for he found employment as a railwayman with the local railway company which later become the L.M.S. (London Midland and Scottish) Railway Company. His first job was as a "surfaceman," which entailed walking along the railway line to check the track and keep it in good repair. I was told he had to buy his own shovel, which he used to move the track stones around the railway lines. Later, he worked as a signalman in various signal boxes between Edinburgh and Montrose, then at Lunan Bay station, and finally at Montrose North. I learned only recently that my granddad had etched his name on a signalbox window, and that my dad—a generation later—also had etched his name on the same window.

James Murray, my grandfather, had two brothers: Robert (Black Watch, killed in

A railway family: my granddad (left) and my dad (right) in their railway uniforms.

August 1918 in France) and William. All were sons of Jane Murray, who is buried at Lunan Church along with husband, Robert Blacklaws. Was he the father of Jane's three children?

When I think of it, there is evidence that my mother and father did have a church upbringing in those small country hamlets and villages, resulting in them experiencing a limited geographical scope. I recall mum telling me that, before they were married, she and my father had an exciting day-trip by train to the Empire Exhibition in Glasgow in 1938. What an amazing experience that must have been for them to escape, even for one day, from the restrictions of life in the country. That trip is a glimpse, for me, of their outward-looking and adventurous spirit which they pursued throughout their life.

So, with my father's family background of ownership of a smiddy and mum's experience of learning her Ps and Qs as a maid and cook in nearby Dunninald Castle, it is not surprising that they had been schooled relatively well, and church was part of their lives. They were clever, well-mannered, and tidy people. All this is why I now come to the point of saying it is not surprising they sought out a church connection for their future family life. Around the time when they married in Montrose on 9th December 1939, dad had applied for a job on the railway at Usan Station. However, this was unsuccessful, but he was told of a job as railway porter/signalman at Monifieth which he accepted. You can imagine the excitement and nervousness of leaving their respective homes when they married and immediately had the added thrill of moving to a strange place with basically only the clothes they could carry.

Their first home together was a rented room at 89 Brook Street, Monifieth. In 1940, when my father was posted to Barry Railway Station as a porter/signalman, they moved to rented room(s) in the bungalow (Somerville) next door to Barry Schoolhouse. I was born at Somerville in October 1940, and my brother James (Peem) was also born there in November 1941. It was there, in the summer of that year, that my uncle Jim (dad's brother) visited, and evidently laid a lucky silver threepenny piece on my pram before going off to El Alamein, where he was killed on the first night of the battle in October.

Sometime in 1943 or 1944 we moved to Annfield Cottage, situated on Barry Road, Carnoustie, where my sister Isobel was born on 26th July 1944. I was christened at Craig Church (my mother's church) near Montrose in December 1940. I can only imagine the tiring day when they travelled the return trip by bus in winter to get home to Monifieth. I think they must have joined Barry Church sometime around 1941–42, when Peem was Christened. I can remember, as a Sunday school pupil aged about 5 years, attending church and leaving the service before the sermon to stand on the stone steps leading to the church hall.

We moved to Anchor Place, Admiral Street, in the winter of 1946/47, and experienced the infamous 1947 serious winter snowstorm. As mentioned earlier, I certainly recall walking home from Carnoustie School along the High Street with snow piled up to a height well above my head. I am quite certain mum and dad had joined Newton Panbride Church fairly soon after moving to Westhaven. I have a picture of Peem and myself on stage in a Sunday school concert, and we looked like six or seven-year olds.

Newton Panbride Church holds many memories for me. Progressing from Sunday School to Youth Fellowship, and then as a regular in many of the Dramatic Club stage presentations, are pleasant recollections. My experiences in the drama group gave me great confidence in my later life to stand up and speak as well as teach. At some point, dad became an elder. He was a quiet man and, looking back, he conducted himself in an unassuming manner. For a short period, when aged about 20, I became a Deacon which entailed visiting church members in their homes in my allotted area, which was Carnoustie west end.

I have very fond memories of Sunday School picnics when we—children, mums and dads—were transported to The Guynd (a country house and garden near Arbroath) or Crombie Park on a trailer pulled by a tractor. Christmas parties were equally happy. They were held in the hall now referred to as Newton Hall (the more recent larger hall is Panbride Hall), and were very well attended. Santa Claus, we were told by teachers as we were teasingly "held back" in the hall, was reportedly "landing by helicopter in the manse garden," and eventually we each got to meet him and received a gift from his large toy sack. We were privileged children.

"Mum and dad practised their family life in a Christian and unassuming way!"

Sunday School, Bible Class and Youth Fellowship

"Not quite the teddy-bear's picnic!"

My earliest memories of Newton Panbride church and Sunday School were the Sunday School gatherings held in what is, today, the "Session Room." It was 1947, and there must have been around ten or fifteen pupils aged between 5 and 11 years old sitting on small folding chairs. One of the songs we sang then was "Pitter patter, pitter patter on the windowpane." (Presumably on wet Sundays?) After The Rev. Mr John Cumming's ministerial address to the children, we were able to leave the church prior to the sermon to join the Sunday School class, and then be met by parents when the church service ended.

Sunday School

When I was twelve years of age, my Sunday School meetings were held in the church after the service. Probably around 20 or 25 pupils gathered in the first two or three pews to be given a talk by the then-Sunday School Superintendent, Mr Steve Ireland, after which there was a prayer. I recall the organist was a Mr Cruickshank. After an introduction by Mr Ireland, classes were split into age groups with boys and girls being separated. Each group met in a defined area with a teacher, for example in areas such as the east and west "pews," and at various spots spread across the central section of the church. One Christmas John Robb and I, then aged 12, were asked to sing a "Silent Night" duet during an evening church service.

Bible Class

Later, aged between about 12 and 15 years, we were in a group numbering around twelve. Described as the "Bible Class," it was led by Mr Chambers who lived in Church Street. After the church service this group met in the church hall and, on (the rare) sunny, warm summer days, under the apple tree on the Manse lawn.

Youth Fellowship

When I was 15, 16 and 17 years of age, I attended a Sunday Evening Youth Fellowship meeting—numbering around 20 or so—who, unlike the earlier groups, were not all Newton Panbride church attendees. This group was initially led by the Minister, who gave us a talk, read a passage, and led a prayer. On occasions, he invited "outside" speakers to give us a talk on a variety of topics—one, I recall, was a talk by Dudley D. Watkins: the famous sketch artist of D.C. Thomson characters *The Broons* and *Oor Willie*.

A typical Sunday evening was to meet in St Bride's Hall (at the corner of Maule Street and Carlogie Road) at 7 pm. After a cup of tea at the end of the evening I, along with my pals, usually stopped off at Tommy Swan's ice cream parlour for a hot orange drink and to play a few records on the jukebox. Later, we would walk along to David Moir's chip shop (opposite the school playground, and beside the very large tree then located in the centre of the pavement) and sit in his café to enjoy yet another hot orange drink—again, with the plan of playing the jukebox and, of course, to check out which girls were around to chat with. All very innocent pastimes for sixteen to seventeen year olds in those days.

Looking back, it is surprising to realise how much we were influenced by the church at that time.

Parties and Picnics

Writing in 2025, Newton Panbride has two church halls. The latest and larger of the two is known as Panbride Hall. In all my childhood days there was only Newton Hall, where I enjoyed so much fun.

Sunday School Christmas Parties

My earliest experience was when I was on stage, aged about 8 and dressed in my pyjamas, in a sketch called "Christopher Robin is Saying His Prayers." In another later sketch, called "The Teddy Bears' Picnic," I was one of several bears dressed in "onesy" costumes made out of clean sacking material.

In addition to those early-stage experiences, the annual Christmas party was also held in Newton Hall. Always good fun, with games and treats. Santa Claus miraculously appeared each year. I recall, after a hush in the games, being told to sit in a circle as it was about the time Santa was going to appear. I also remember that two Sunday School teachers, George Spalding and John Fox, were posted outside the hall to give us word of Santa's approach. Now and again, they opened the hall door to say that Santa hadn't arrived yet. And then the magic news was announced that his helicopter had landed on the church manse garden! From that moment we were kept up to date with his movements, until finally he announced his arrival by loud knocking on the hall door. What fun! Gifts were dispensed by name, and we all went happily home. (And we even believed the helicopter story!)

Sunday School Picnics

Each year, sometime around the Easter period was when the annual Sunday School picnic took place. I think my first Newton Panbride Picnic outing was to The Guynd, a park somewhere near Arbroath, but I have clearer memories of successive picnics at Crombie Park.

The mode of transport from the church to the park was quite basic. Parents and their children (and, in some cases, unaccompanied children) were accommodated on farm trailers (or bogeys), sometimes with our feet dangling over the side of the trailer. Usually, the base of the bogey was covered in clean Hessian, and draped around the trailer was colourful paper or fabric decorations. The excitement was intense—to have a ride or "hurl" on the bogey was one thing, but to be pulled along by a petrol-smelling tractor puffing out black exhaust smoke added to the fun. Health and safety regulations didn't exist then, but gradually lorries with sides were introduced. The journey to Crombie must have taken around 45 minutes, and while mums and dads and some smaller children went to the rhododendron-enclosed picnic area, I recall—along with my friends—heading directly to the edge of the reservoir.

I visited the picnic area and the embankment around the reservoir in 2024, and I was delighted to see that the features of the exact area had not changed. What fascinated us boys in those early days was the massive "hatch" of tadpoles which, each year, frequented the water's edge. When we became so engrossed with the spectacle,

Sunday School teachers appeared and urged us to get ready for the races. There were categories for all. Boys and girls took part in a "dash" of 100 yards, an egg and spoon race, and wheelbarrow and three-legged races. Even mums and dads had a chance to run. Once the races were over, each person was handed a paper bag containing one or two sandwiches, a cake and a drink—usually a small bottle of lemonade. Then it was back to the tadpoles, followed by the exciting hurl home on the "bogey."

"Dinna stand up in the trailer while we're moving!"

Newton Panbride Dramatic Club

"How do you manage to remember all those words!" (Mum's words when I got home after each show.)

The fact I ended up on the stage of Newton Panbride Church Hall was a pure piece of luck. (Well, it was for me!) My school friend Willie Yool was an apprentice in the Edward and Ramsay joinery business located in premises on the east side of Ferrier Street. He was making great progress and hugely enjoying his evening classes as well as the building/construction theory content of his studies. Without much discussion, and for reasons unknown, he went off to join the Royal Navy. When he came home on leave, we always enjoyed good fun. In those days, military and naval personnel wore uniform in civilian surroundings, and Willie was so very proud of his matelot uniform and knew the girls we met were impressed.

One evening we didn't like the prospect of the film being shown at the Regal cinema and walked along to the Pavilion in Park Avenue, only to find it closed as there was a play being presented by Newton Panbride Dramatic Club. We ventured in and, to my amazement, saw on stage during the play my Scout Master John Fox, my Sunday School teacher Steve Ireland, and a few other well-known faces including George Spalding (a salesman) Norman McDonald (a fruit and veg retailer) Bertha Robson (a teacher), Florence Petrie (another teacher) and Mina Mackay (daughter of the Mackay's jam factory owner).

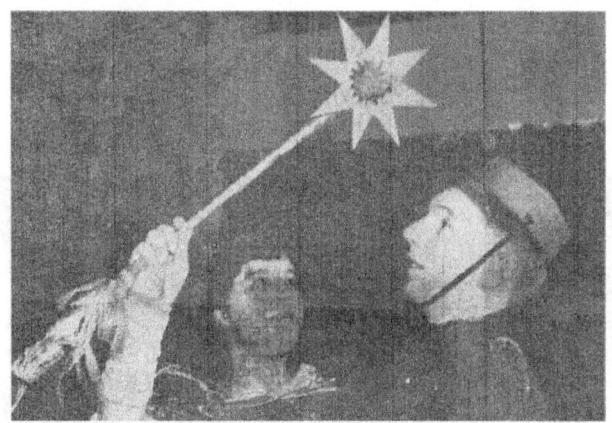

Newton Panbride Dramatic Club—my last part, as Buttons, which turned out to be "curtains" for me!

I immediately felt the allure and wanted to be part of the club. Later, I accidentally met John Fox and chatted about the play, and I discussed my keen desire to be on stage. He invited me along to the next available club meeting. My love affair with amateur drama had started—and I never missed a Friday evening meeting for rehearsals.

My first part, when I was 17 years old, was as Hopcroft Minor in the three-act farce *The Happiest Days of Your Life*. Later, I was to be involved in several one-act plays. I met my wife-to-be, Gail Jamieson, who had later joined the club, and I went on to take up larger main parts playing opposite her and involving screeds of words to learn. *House by the Lake*, *Sailor Beware*, and *Love from a Stranger* are a few parts I recall, and I even went on to direct the three-act Oscar Wilde play *Lord Arthur Savile's Crime*.

Sadly, my last performance for the club was in 1961 as Buttons in our one and only pantomime to be held in St Bride's Hall in Carlogie Road. My amazing luck that night of finding the Pavilion cinema closed had led me on to overcome my shyness with girls, general conversation, and it certainly helped me cope with my first class of students at Dundee Commercial College in 1963. My dramatic club experience was a helpful chapter which proved to be a valuable stepping stone throughout my working life.

"I learned a few valuable lessons!"

A Murray family gathering in 1989.
From L to R: Isobel, Robbie, Dad, James (Peem), Mum, Jean.

CHAPTER 5

My Family

My Dad and the Railway

"It didn't seem like it at the time, but the railway company was like a family!"

While growing up, I was aware merely that my father worked on "the Railway," was always on shifts (early or late), and that he had to travel to his workplace "under his own steam." I suppose not seeing his workplace or any colleagues, and hearing no discussion at home about his work or his employer, led me to simply accept that he came and went rather silently. Although we lived within 200 yards of the main Aberdeen-London railway line and witnessed so many famous steam engines, my impressions were of "the railway" as being some kind of remote and impersonal employer. Of course, I knew my dad's original rail employer was N.B. (North British), followed by L.M.S. (London, Midland and Southern), then L.N.E.R. (London & North-East Rail Company), followed by B.R. (British Rail), the nationalised company. I knew passengers and goods were transported but, growing up in the 1950s, I had a critical view of the operation—rough, uneven platforms (especially in high profile stations such as King's Cross, London), and poorly and untidily-dressed porters pushing rickety, noisy and ancient ungainly wheelbarrows. Food sold at stations was greatly criticised, and in general the operation had a very poor image and reputation—although, to be fair, the trains ran on time. Looking back to those early years, it's fair to say that my view of my dad's employer was quite dim.

Noticeably, over the decades, standards improved with steam engines replaced by diesel or electric, cleaner coaches, and well dressed and better trained staff. It was during the Covid-19 lockdowns that I ventured into my loft and tried to make a start to inspect and tidy old papers. Subsequently I have been able to put together the history of how my father and his own father were each employed for their respective lifetimes on the railway.

My grandfather was born near Brechin, and worked on farms before he started work as a 'surface man' on the N.B. (North British) Railway, with a weekly wage of 18 shillings—out of which (as mentioned elsewhere in this book) he had to purchase his own work shovel. On 15th April 1909, his 21st birthday, he commenced work as a porter at Lunan Bay Railway Station with a pay packet of 20 shillings (one pound) per week. He completed 44 years of service on the railways in 1953.

Initially, in 1937, my father worked as a "length man" (surfaceman) with L.M.S. (London Midland and Southern) Railway Company at Lauriston then at Monifieth, in 1940, as a porter/signalman, before becoming a regular signalman. In time, L.M.S. became L.N.E.R. (London and North-East Rail) and eventually B.R. (British Rail). I wish I had asked him for his detailed training "theory" notes. I once had an opportunity to look at his jotters full of "railway procedures." The detail looked highly technical, and of course all based on safe working practices.

I think he could have remained as a signalman for as long as he wished, but pay would be better if he worked as a "relief signalman." After introductory training in many different signal boxes, he was employed to work—often at short notice—in signal boxes within an area stretching from Invergowrie to Lunan Bay, and across the River Tay to Wormit. This in itself was a demanding job, but his problem was compounded by the fact he had to reach every location on his push-bike.

Several memories remain with me. On one occasion, on 5th January 1979, he cycled to Invergowrie in a snowstorm to facilitate the Aberdeen/London train passing through. (I have a letter from his British Rail manager thanking him for his Herculean effort in the snow! Then, on another winter's day, I recall seeing him set off on his bike. He showed me his gloved hands, when I found the palms of his gloves were worn bare. Times were hard, and I know the first thing he had to do when he arrived at the signal box in early winter mornings was to light the fire and occasionally dry out his soaked clothing. Luckily, he had a good supply of coal, for he once told me firemen on steam trains would regularly, on request, drop off lumps of coal when passing by.

With no travel allowance to cover his expenses, including the cost of batteries for his old-fashioned bicycle lamps, it was essential that he kept his bike in reliable working order. However, on one occasion his bike let him down, and he had to suffer a ride as pillion on my motor bike to Lunan Bay to arrive before 6am. That was probably one of his worst ever journeys to a signal box. In time, he managed to buy himself an Excelsior motor bike, which unfortunately ran with a fuel mixture thus causing unending problems until he eventually bought a second-hand Vespa scooter—what a treat that must have been! By the time he approached retirement, he had the luxury of a small car.

4th L.N.E.R. Battalion, HOME GUARD.

WHAT YOU **MUST** DO WHEN THE HOME GUARD IS CALLED OUT.

1. Put on uniform and take the whole of your arms and equipment to the place where you have been instructed to report.
2. Bring the undermentioned articles with you:—
   (a) Enough food to last 24 hours, drinking mug and plate or mess tin, with knife, fork and spoon.
   (b) Razor, lather brush, hairbrush and comb, towel, soap, toilet paper.
   (c) Spare pair of socks, handkerchiefs. (Have a rucksack or sand bag ready to hold the above.)
   (d) Identity Card bearing Battalion Stamp.
   (e) **Your own** Ration Books.
   (f) Notebook and pencil.
   (g)
   (h)
3. Keep this part of the form and CHECK OVER when called out.
4. Fill in the following details and hand the slip to your Platoon Officer **when called out.**

NOT TO BE DETACHED UNTIL CALLED OUT.

NAME.. NAT. 'REG. No..................

ADDRESS... RANK...............................

COMPANY.................. PLATOON.................. DATE..................

TO BE HANDED TO PLATOON OFFICER ON REPORTING FOR DUTY WHEN CALLED OUT.

My dad's 4th L.N.E.R. Home Guard duty recruitment instruction form.

He clocked up 42 years' service, during which time he was a member of the National Union of Railwaymen and had been a member of the 4th Battalion L.N.E.R. Home Guard during WW2. Having had the opportunity to look through old letters, I have now formed an enlightened view of his lifelong employer. The respect, gratitude and admiration expressed in letters by senior managers towards my father and grandfather for their long and faithful service is touching. I have totally revised my view of what I once thought was a distant and remote employer.

Amongst the papers I found are records of the many signal boxes where my father and grandfather were employed during their respective service, and it is so clear how small villages deep in the countryside were linked by rail to the national network. Mainly because my father and grandfather were both quiet, unassuming men who calmly went about their demanding work, I—as a young person—viewed the railway company as a remote, impersonal and mysterious organisation. Luckily, I have now been able to see his employer in a more favourable light.

Helping Dad in his Garden

"It's time to 'prick' out the neeps, Robert. Leave one every nine inches!"

Both mum and dad had grown up in the countryside. Mum at Boddin near Usan by Montrose, and dad at Lunan Bay—thus providing each with a spacious family vegetable garden. They brought with them to Carnoustie not only their shared church background but additional practical elements of their country life. Their idea was to keep hens and rabbits, and make productive use of their ground space. It followed that my father cultivated and greatly enjoyed a vegetable garden wherever he lived—namely at Annfield Cottages at Barry Road, Anchor Place at Westhaven, and at 4 Shamrock Street, Carnoustie. His ideas helped to see them through the war years.

I grew up with an awareness of how important a garden was—particularly a vegetable garden for growing produce for use at home. When I visited both grandparents' homes, I always joined my dad and my granddads as they walked around their vegetable gardens. I listened intently to the various comments about how "things were doing"—well, or less well—which were invariably accompanied by some reason or excuse, but always instructive for me. I picked up the jargon relating to the weather, the poor seed, the condition of the soil, manure, and good or bad timing of planting. "Aye we had a late frost." "I bought the wrang seed!" "It's no the richt soil here for that!" Consequently, I think I soaked up quite a bit of unwitting learning about what, where, and when to grow each vegetable.

I recall the careful sequence that my father followed. First, to save—over the year—waste food and kitchen scraps in a certain area in the garden, and nearer the time of digging to collect (for his Westhaven plot) a supply of seaweed, which incidentally the local farmer also ploughed into his fields. Using his wheelbarrow, my brother and I helped him collect seaweed when we saw the right type had been washed up on the beach. The ideal seaweed was the small pieces including dulse, which could be buried nicely in the garden trench—unlike the long, hard "tangles" which did not rot so well.

With a supply of seaweed and kitchen waste ready, it was time to dig. He did not simply turn over a spade of soil, but did what he called "double digging." His procedure was to dig a trench the length of his plot at what he called the "start" end of the garden, and move the earth to the "finish" end. Into the trench went, first, the weeds which had grown over the garden since the previous crop had been harvested. He did this by running his spade horizontally under the carpet of weeds and tipping them into the trench. Following this, he then carefully put in a roughly measured amount of seaweed and kitchen waste to sufficiently cover each area to be turned over. Conveying successive barrowloads of seaweed and waste when it was needed, with no delays, was one of my helping tasks in the process. By the time the ground was completely dug over, the area was tidy and the waste products were all under the freshly dug soil. After a week or so, when the ground had settled, he raked over the tilled soil, and then it was time to start planting.

Drills the length or width of the garden patch were prepared, into which went the seed potatoes. One potato was planted every nine inches or so (or the length of the gardener's boot!). I think on some instances he may also have added some blood or bone meal in the furrow. Seed potatoes came with different names and characteristics. Some were better for early crops, and some were better for boiling as opposed to frying. Names I recall were Edzell Blues, Majestics, Dukes of York, Epicures, and Pipers.

My first detailed recollections relate to our Westhaven Garden, where the prime crop each year was potatoes which occupied around half of the available space. Cabbage, Brussels sprouts and cauliflower were planted as "transplants" and not as seeds. Plants, one at a time, were dropped into holes, about twelve inches apart, in the ground—made by a "dibble" stick. Dad bought transplants locally—probably from Pat Birse, the local ironmonger—but occasionally he may have had some gifted by his father. It was important to know where you could source good quality transplants.

Lettuce, carrots and turnips, on the other hand, were sown as seeds. Dad always had a line stretched across the breadth of his patch, and at intervals of around eighteen inches to two feet, he created grooves in the soil into which he trickled in a line of seeds straight from the small paper bag he had purchased them in. When the carrots and turnips were "infant" shoots, he then pricked out some shoots and discarded them, leaving one shoot every few inches to develop into a fully-grown plant. (Where entire fields of turnip seeds were sown, the farmer engaged a squad of workers to "thin out" the small shoots. In the farming world, this was described as "clattin' the neeps"—in other words, thinning out and discarding the unnecessary turnip seedlings. Small lettuce shoots could be left to grow, or be thinned out. Dad trained me on how to thin out, and it was a satisfying task.

Dad had a clever way of storing potatoes in a box of straw kept in the shed, away from the frost. In the case of carrots, he—each year—dug a pit in the garden and filled it with dry sand, in which he stored the carrots. A metal or wooden lid over the pit helped to keep fresh carrots available well into the winter.

My favourite routine was planting peas. This entailed quite a specific procedure. Again keeping a gap between his lines of plants or seeds, dad used the width of his spade to create a shallow, two-inch deep channel into which peas, from a packet, were carefully placed around, two or three inches apart. The trench was then gently covered over with soil, and gently "patted down" using the back of a spade. Unlike all other seedlings and transplants, peas (and beans) required careful assistance to grow. They were "climbing" plants, and stakes had to be placed around each side of the trench onto which he attached a net or wire-netting to encourage the plants to grow up to around two or three feet high. One of my tasks was to place a small wooden stake at the end of each row, with the seed packet wrapped around it so that it was clear to know not only what had been planted, but where. Placed at intervals around the garden patch were longer stakes or bamboo canes, onto which were attached strips of silver paper, streamers, or whirling items to help scare away unwelcome seed-eating birds.

My joy of watching the progress of dad's garden produce develop through the ground and up to maturity is one of my favourite memories. I felt I had been part of the process to get freshly-picked garden produce on to our lunch table. When vegetables appeared on my dinner plate, I felt a real sense of satisfaction in having been part of the procedure.

"Aye, a satisfying way of keeping fit and saving money!"

A Visit to Woodside Croft

"Dinna forget to put on your nicky tams!"

Elsewhere in this stroll down Memory Lane, I have mentioned special Easter and Christmas visits to my mother's parents' croft situated on Dunninald Castle estate, near Montrose. But I would like to give here a more general impression of the croft and its environs.

Perhaps, initially, I should say that for as long as I can remember my grandfather, George Taylor—born and raised at Guthrie near Friockhiem—resided in the Croft cottage with his wife, my granny Anne Hutcheson, who originated at Tigerton, near Little

Brechin. I have seen early photographs of me as an infant in the cottage garden, which gave me some indication that they were residing there in 1940.

But in fact, only in 2023 my cousin Anne (the daughter of my mum's twin sister) provided me with letters indicating that granddad had, prior to terminating his employment as grieve at Boddin Farm, leased the croft from the Dunninald Castle Estate (owned by the Stansfelds family) for £17 p.a. in 1929, and had remained in it until his death. Only recently I have found an old photograph of George Taylor with his mother. That's the only great-grandparent picture I have.

From L to R: My grandfather, his son (my uncle) Alan, my great granny, and Alan's daughter June (my cousin). The photo was possibly taken in 1929, around the time when granddad took over the croft.

My granny attended to all domestic matters: feeding hens, collecting eggs, cooking, and distributing food for the three or four pigs which they kept in sties as well as looking after and milking Maisie the cow. I now realise that my mum and her brothers and sisters must have been aware of the relatively higher status that their father had achieved by advancing from farm manager to the rank of self-sufficient crofter.

I recall, on visits, seeing granddad scatter seed, crop manure and lime in "Biblical style" by hand on his fields, using a large canvas tray protruding from his waist and held up by straps over his shoulders. I still remember helping at harvest time and watching the horse-powered "binder" with its revolving paddle wheel gather the grain, then cut it before tying it in sheaves with string and then ejecting them at regular spots along the field. Each sheaf was roughly equivalent to what could be gathered under-arm by a person. Sheaves were then collected and, at intervals along the field, four sheaves were set up to lean on another four sheaves (sometimes six leaning on six) to form a tent-like structure which was described as a "stook." This allowed drying until later, when all the dried sheaves were loaded on to a trailer (or bogey) and taken to the croft farmyard where they were built into stacks. Stacks were roughly 15 feet high and eight or ten feet in diameter, and finished on top with a cone shape finish with a canvas thatch, held down by ropes or a net, to protect them from rain. Granddad always seemed to produce two stacks which stood for a month or so until it was time for threshing.

It seemed to me and my brother Peem that everything was so well thought-out and organised. Timing of the threshing must have been determined by the weather—and granddad's availability. Then the final piece of a season's grain production came when the threshing machine, or "thresher," arrived.

Like all the other elements of the harvest gathering, the thresher—almost the size of a double-decker bus—seemed magically to accept sheaves at the top and produce corn or wheat grains at one end and waste (called straw) at the other. This ingenious machine produced its own excitement. I have no detailed knowledge of what the circuit was, but the local farmers seemed to have a system of sharing the "thresher," and each farm in turn had the use of the machine and two or three men with it. Granddad, being a small crofter/producer, was probably last in the queue each year.

Once the thresher was in place alongside a stack, three men would climb to the top of the stack to remove the thatch. One man cut the string around each sheaf, and then—with the aid of a long-handled pitchfork—two men threw sheaves into the thresher. While each stack was being threshed, a ring of netting wire—about three or four feet high—was placed around the entire stack. This was the most exciting part of the threshing procedure for, as threshing progressed, the stack diminished and rats began to escape the danger of their shrinking home. It was then clear to me why granddad's two dogs had been placed inside the surrounding wire. Say no more! This was also when I realised why the three men while working on top of the stack had string tied tightly around their trousers below the knee. The term for the trousers worn in such a manner was "nicky tams"—obviously to prevent a "nick" from a disgruntled rat. When sheaves had been threshed and the grain seeds separated, the straw was then stored in a long, high stack called a "straw-soo" with an overlaid, roped-down canvas cover. Straw was important as bedding for granny's cow and pigs.

Life on the croft offered so many interesting jobs. This included collecting buckets of crystal-clear cold water from the deep well 200 yards down the road from the cottage, and collecting eggs from the hen houses. (Hens which didn't want to part with their egg(s) were described as "cloakers." They would peck angrily when an attempt was made to remove an egg from under them.) Then there was helping to carry buckets of pig food to the sties, picking soft fruits from

My grandfather cutting grain with a binder.

the garden, and cutting grass on the front "Victorian" lawn. I learned so much on my visits to the croft.

Adding to those day-time chores was the evening walk with granddad while he checked his snares around the perimeter of the three fields. Not surprisingly, we found trapped rabbits and hares—some still alive. Sad and horrible, but part of real countryside life. A cruel end for some animals, but part of country life survival.

Tattie-picking was another chore. Grandad had his own tattie-digger, described as a "spider," so described because it spun around like a spinning wheel with forks attached while pulled along behind a tractor to dig out potatoes. Our fun on early, dark October evenings was to roast potatoes in a fire of burning tattie shaws. Many other wonderful play-days were spent outdoors in good weather—trapping birds under a "riddle" (sieve) propped up by a stick, and sometimes playing on the swing which granddad had rigged up on the rafters of the big shed. Wet days provided equally absorbing pursuits when we played granny's table-top gramophone almost continuously as we enjoyed our favourite 78s (vinyl records played at 78 r.p.m.). There was everything from Robert Wilson's *Down in the Glen* to Bing Crosby singing *Beautiful Dreamer*.

Without doubt, holidays at the croft were amongst the most satisfying experiences of my life. It's where I was filled with a sense of the changing seasons, and unwittingly learned a work ethic. When I started to read, learn, and write about the life of Robert Burns, I came to realise that the life of my gran and granddad had must have been little changed from that experienced by Scotland's National Bard. When I studied Burns' works at school, I found it easy to relate to what he wrote. I now realise that my granddad probably observed his father and grandfather carrying out jobs "on the land" in a form or style that was little changed from Burns' time.

"Come on now, lads—time to check the snares!"

My Essay about Uncle Tom

"Come, Tommo—I give you ride around the city!"

The open-top Edinburgh City Tours double-decker bus trundled slowly down the city's cobbled High Street, also known as The Royal Mile. Passengers, no doubt pleased with the gentle pace on a summer's morning, would acknowledge that the driver was in no hurry to do his job. After all, he could stop and start anywhere on his route and none of his supervisors would be aware. The young driver sounded the old-fashioned rasping horn, and the wee elderly man seated on the outdoors bench lowered his newspaper, returned a brisk wave and toddled ungainly, as fast as his short legs would take him, onto the lower deck and directly to the seat immediately behind the man at the wheel.

Before I take you further on my story, I ought to reveal that "the wee elderly man" is my Uncle Tom. For me, he was a rather remote character in my life, but over the years I heard from my mother and father interesting snippets about him. Those small, important pieces of information are reflected in my tribute to him—although to help illustrate Tom's remarkable life, I have invented the dialogue which is shown in italics.

"Morning, Tommo. How you this day?"

"Fine, fine, Stefan. What a bonny mornin'."

"Have no' seen you for while, Tommo. You okay?"

"Legs been bad, Stefan."

"No worries. Danny, no at work today. Just tell Davy upstairs I say you can sit up top—no charge. How many trips you like today, Tommo?"

"Thank you, Stefan. It's good—no showers forecast. So maybe two or three circuits."

"Relax and enjoy, Tommo. I sign off 1500 hrs."

Tom, known as Tommo by Stefan the Polish immigrant driver, made his way adeptly upstairs, grasping the handrails to pull himself up to his accustomed look-out post.

"So Danny's AWOL, is he?" he said to the conductor. "I'm Tom; a regular. Stefan knows me. This is my usual seat," Tom announced with characteristically charming cheekiness.

"Aye, nae problem, pal," replied the conductor with casual acceptance. "I'm Davy."

Tom, comfortable in his customary seat—third row from the back on the left—sat back and pondered his luck.

"What's so special about that seat then, Tom?" Davy asked.

"Ah, you see—I know more places where I worked on this side of the route, and there's less flies and fumes here!"

Davy attended intermittently to his passengers on the bus, and there developed a conversation between the two at intervals. Tom, most of the time in his own world, was an observer of people and places, and his circuits gave him a bird's eye view of the various past chapters of his life in the city.

"How did you come to get free rides then, Tom?" enquired Davy curiously.

"It was easy. One day—a bit like today—Stefan's bus was gridlocked on the Mile, and per chance got bogged down in the traffic exactly at the gate of my residence: Whitefoord House."

"Ooh, a residence?" Davy quizzed with the tone of being impressed.

"Yes, you see, I've gone up in the world!" Tom joked with a broad grin. "You know, it's a home for retired military veterans like me, and I was lucky to be allocated a room. I'd been sitting on the bench beside the front door, and I could see the driver was agitated. So, I went across and chatted. I jokingly told him not to worry; I knew the city like the back of my hand, and he said jump in. That's how it started."

Tom wouldn't have been conscious of his own natural curiosity, but that was no doubt what took him to engage the driver in conversation—after all, Tom did know the capital well, and he probably thought he could give the friendly foreign driver some valuable advice. That was Tom's way. Not nosey or invasive; merely inquisitive and chatty, in the way that a gentle, clever, lonely old man would behave.

"Look, Davy—over there. That's the convent where I was billeted as the live-in gardener for twenty-five years."

"Well done. Has it changed much, do you think?"

"I'll say! You see that line of leylandii firs? They must be 30 feet high. Well, that was one of my first jobs. I planted them as saplings. Management gave me free rein. I laid everything out as I wanted; bought all the plants and shrubs. When we turn the next corner, you'll see the rose beds I created."

"What a great job to have. You must enjoy seeing it all."

"In a way. But you can see the roses are not being properly pruned, and the lawns need feeding."

Davy attended to his customers, and Tom's mind went back to the job he did without interference. He recalled his retirement party, when everyone said their farewells. He knew he was highly respected there at the convent. His tour continued, and took him past the spacious gardens of his wealthy clients whose gardens he cared for on a self-employed basis after his convent days. He occasionally would call out with glee the names of his clients.

"Look, Davy! You see that grand grey stone Victorian villa in its wooded grounds? That was one of my biggest regular jobs. That was Professor Purves' home. Used to get good bonuses there, and his wife saw that the maid always had a tray of tea and homemade cakes ready for me."

"Lucky you, Tom!" smiled the conductor.

"And, in a minute, if you look across the road in a few hundred yards, you'll see another nice place where I worked. You see that red sandstone bungalow? That was Doctor Davidson's place. He knew the Latin name for every flower and plant in his garden. We both learned from each other."

"Was it hard work, Tom?"

"Not really, I enjoyed the people, and I worked whatever hours they wanted."

On his circuits, Tom's "sharp eye" would assess every minute detail and how changes—"not all for the better"—had been introduced. Public parks and even Princes Street Gardens, although never his responsibility, were also under his severe regular scrutiny. While employed in the convent, he had enjoyed quality lodgings, but during those later working years he shared a Morningside bungalow with other men who worked in the city. By then, Tom was too old to venture out and about, and he became the guardian of the property when the others had gone out to work. He kept the coal fire alive and well—keeping the place warm in winter—and he became the general handyman. It was when that shared arrangement ended that Tom successfully obtained a place at Whitefoord House.

His thoughts, while gazing expertly all around from his eagles' nest position, took him beyond his Edinburgh days—back home, far back to where he grew up at Lunan Bay, near Montrose. He recalled his happy, carefree boyhood days of growing up in the family home, the Station Master's house, and adventuring along the clifftops and sandy beaches as well as fishing for brown trout in Lunan Water.

"Were you always a gardener then Tom?" Davy asked him.

"Except for the war years. It was pure luck that I lived beside the Blair-Imrie gentry—the long-standing owners of Lunan House mansion. The Blair-Imries had money, and it was my good fortune that they were looking for a willing gardening boy to serve his apprenticeship on their lawns and gardens. I learned about everything: flowers, vegetables, fruit trees, and bushes. I got to know some of the maids as well!"

"I'll bet you did—you old rascal!"

As his personal tour at the hands of his friend Stefan coincidentally took Tom past Leith Docks, he recalled the day he reported as required at the recruiting office in Montrose High Street and, to his surprise, found himself returning to his parents to report he was to be called up to the 'Senior Service". He recalled the recruiting officer's firm and clear decision: "You're a seaside lad—you'll know what the sea looks like. So it's the Navy for you, my boy."

"What did you do in wartime then, Tom?" Davy asked, picking up the thread of the conversation.

"When I was nearing my 27th birthday," Tom replied, "I was called up and found myself on a ship—nothing special."

(Records found by me are sparse, but enough to tell me his rank was Able Bodied Seaman, and he had been aboard the *Grenville*—a land-based dormitory in Sierra Leone (such bases were often referred to as "stone-wall frigates") and later crewed on HMS *Pursuer*. My father told me that Tom had, twice, had to abandon ship, though for whatever reason I'm not certain. However, it seems that Tom spent considerable time in the water—luckily in semi-tropical seas.

It was Tom who, on learning that the Black Watch had sailed from Liverpool and were ashore from SS *Empress of Australia* in Sierra Leone harbour, made a dramatic plea to be allowed ashore to meet with his younger brother, Jim. Evidently, they were allowed one hour together—neither had any idea where they were bound—but it was the last sixty minutes they were to enjoy together, for Jim died less than three months later on the first night of the barrage at El Alamein. Tom reflected on that sad day: his brother's farewell to life, and yet here he was—unfairly, he felt, on a bus safe with his war experiences securely behind him and enjoying the city he loved. (He couldn't get out of his mind that, by some strange quirk, his brother Jim had been batman to Colonel Blair-Imrie of Lunan.)

"What a small world," he voiced without thinking.

Uncle Tom back during his Royal Navy service as an Able Bodied Seaman.

"You've been very quiet, Tom. Are you alright?"

"Just thinking about some of the old days," he muttered. In truth, it was young Jim he was thinking of, but it was too painful a memory to recount to a stranger—even a friendly one. As the High Street came into view on the second circuit, Tom made his way gingerly downstairs to the seat behind his driver friend.

"Going off early today, Tommo? Only two circuits?"

"Yes. What a wonderful day, Stefan. Going for a lie down before tea. Thanks again. You take care now!" he said as he departed.

"What a funny wee man, Stefan," remarked Davy when he took a moment later to chat.

"There's something about him—full of stories, and he has sharp mind. Always cheery."

As Tom waved goodbye, little did he know that summer's day was to be his last carefree city tour with the kind-hearted Stefan. Tom's legs became more of a problem, and they finally gave out. During his next winter he was taken, coincidentally, into the Murray Care Home where, on arrival, he cheerfully remarked to matron: "Would you believe it—I'm home at last!"

Several months later, he died alone in his sleep in the early hours of the morning of 26th July 1993—his 81st year. It seemed evident by the items found on the floor at the side of his bed that they were those he had looked at before falling asleep—photos of his *Grenville* and *Pursuer* sailing mates (he would have known all the names), his gardening record book of accounts, and his gardener's diary.

The care assistants told us he had been singing—while seated—at a Saturday evening party a week before he passed away, and that too was no surprise. At family anniversary events over the years, it was Tom who stood up and sang his repertoire of Scottish songs—including at my mother and father's family gatherings in the Royal British Legion function room in Carnoustie.

Although I have found some interesting love letters from "Evelyn"—evidently an admirer—Tom never married. He was a chatty, cheerful, yet sad wee man, and when he came on holiday to Carnoustie for his annual summer holiday to live with my mum and dad, he amazed us all by turning up with what he proudly called (in naval terms) his "tiddly case"—the smallest case imaginable, in which he had packed his holiday essentials. (He still referred to holiday as "leave"). Each year, my mum was horrified to imagine what the well-polished brown case didn't contain, and would not have been overjoyed to find out. Only Tom, who had solo navigated his way around his world, knew the answer.

Thomas Edwards Murray was born on 7th December 1912. His letters, photos and personal belongings are contained, along with a copy of this story, in his brown "tiddly" case referred to in the story—the one he always used when he travelled to Carnoustie for his "leave."

My Family and Wars

Several members of my family were involved in the defence of the nation during the tumultuous global events of the twentieth century.

My Great Uncle Bob was Killed in France

Jim Murray, my grandfather, had two brothers named Robert and William. I have never heard anything of William, but I know that Robert (Bob), my great uncle, was killed aged 28 on 1st August 1918 in Flanders, France, where he served as a Sergeant in the Black Watch.

All three boys were born out of wedlock, as their parents—for reasons unknown—never married until 1896, and their mother Jane Murray is buried in Lunan churchyard with her husband (and the father?) John Blacklaws.

My grandad's brother Bob Murray in Black Watch uniform.

My Uncle Tom was Shipwrecked Twice

Uncle Tom, having served in the Royal Navy, was shipwrecked twice and survived in foreign seas. He returned to his gardening job at Lunan Bay after the war, then moved to Edinburgh where he worked as a self-employed jobbing gardener until he retired. He was unmarried.

My Uncle Jim was Killed in North Africa

My father's brother, Jim, worked as a joiner and then plumber in Montrose. He was a Black Watch Territorial, and was called up to fight in August 1942, aged 23. Posted to Egypt, he was killed on the first night of the battle at El Alamein. The victory there was what Winston Churchill described as the "end of the beginning" of WW2.

My father's brother, Black Watch Private Jim Murray.

Over the years, I learned a good deal about the war experiences of all three relatives, and in 2007 I travelled to Egypt to visit my uncle Jim's grave at El Alamein. Jim was batman to Colonel Hew Blair-Imrie of Lunan House, Lunan Bay.

I never considered my family as having military history, but of course two World Wars meant mass recruitment and left numerous families like mine with tragic losses.

Cousin Jim: James Ross Murray, B.E.M.

My story of relatives in the Forces is not yet finished, for my father's youngest brother David was a survivor of the Second World War. That uncle, David—who settled in Airdrie after the war—had three sons, the oldest of whom was my cousin Jim (yes, another Jim!) who served as a career soldier in the Royal Marines with great pride and distinction.

To my shame I was only rarely able to meet up with Jim on a few family events, and consequently was largely unaware of his exploits in the Royal Marine commandos. Sadly, it took until his death on 22nd September 2024, and his funeral on 15th October that year, for me to fully comprehend the extent of his distinguished career. Peem and I attended Jim's funeral at Holytown Crematorium, Airdrie, and found the service uplifting and impressive. The cortege was preceded by a Flag Officer and Marine Commandos, and cousin Jim's coffin—draped with a Union Jack on which lay his Green Beret—was laid down while *Hymn to The Fallen* was played by The Central Band of the Royal British Legion.

Army Chaplain Rev Lorraine Gilroy led the service, and spoke of Jim's years of service with 42 Commando in Borneo, Malaysia, Northern Ireland, and the Falklands—later as Flag Officer and then Troop Quartermaster 45 Commando during Mountain and Arctic training in Norway. She recalled Jim's role as Sergeant Major on board HMS *Hermes*, enroute to the South Pacific.

The Chaplain read out a glowing testimonial written by Jim's Commanding Officer, which referred to Jim's distinguished career and mentioned that his well-earned British Empire Medal was the highest honour he could bestow. Jim's faith, courage, and strength of character was highlighted, as well as how he had led by example while fighting for Queen and Country. It was a hugely

My cousin Jim Murray BEM, Royal Marine Commandos.

emotional moment when the Marines' bugler played *Sunset*.

I have lived with great respect for my lost Great Uncle Bob, Uncle Tom and Uncle Jim, whom I never knew and whose photographs in my vestibule I speak to every day. But now I have a man of my generation who I think of every day, and who excelled to his highest level possible. R.I.P., James Ross Murray.

Other Family Members

I had only four Murray cousins, and we rarely saw them as my uncle David's family lived in Lanarkshire. My father's only sister, unmarried, died aged 38 in 1955. "She died on the operating table while undergoing a hernia operation," my dad told me. (This was something that would surely raise some questions in 2025.)

I have been able to read papers and see photographs and put together the family tree of both Taylor and Murray families, and it is quite overwhelming to view how life panned out for my immediate ancestors—a view that they themselves lived through, and yet would never see the whole picture.

Dad enjoying some time with me, Isobel and Peem near Carnoustie Band Stand.

Mum (right), shown with her twin, Jean (left).

CHAPTER 6

My Early Working Life

Delivering Newspapers for Harry Christie

"Would you like a hurl in our car, Robert?"

My mum went into the shop to pay Mr Christie for *The Courier* newspaper, which was delivered every day to our address—Anchor Place, Admiral Street, Westhaven. He asked if her two boys (aged 12 and 11) would be interested in "working" a paper round. Peem and I jumped at the chance— it would mean pocket money for "the pictures" (cinema), lines and hooks for fishing, and saving for scout camp holidays. I pasted wallpaper on an empty two pound can of Tate and Lyle's Golden Syrup, in which I saved my pay and tips.

The paper shop was located at 44 High Street, next to the old Bank of Scotland building and opposite the art-deco building that housed Strachan's Garage (which now, in 2025, is a car park and electric car charging point). We had to start our rounds at 6:45 am at the latest. Some customers worked in Dundee and wanted to read their paper before driving to work or walking to the railway station. If we were soaked to the skin and delayed, it was quite a challenge to change clothing and have breakfast before we dashed off to school.

My "paper round" included Church Street, William Street, Carlogie Road, McKenzie Street, Maule Street, Dalhousie Street, and Guthrie Street, and Peem's covered Arbroath Road, Westhaven, and Tayside Street. Harry wrote addresses on the top of each paper, and where there was more than one newspaper, he folded together all papers and wrote the address on the top paper.

In the early development of properties, in what is now called Carlogie Road, feus were sold in the mid/late 1800s on a 99-year lease, and such owners were nicknamed the "ninety niners". It was the norm in those days to use only the house name. Examples included St Clair, Rimuha, Westfield, Homestead, St Helens, and Corwharn. Alternatively, of course, Harry would use road numbers, but that area had more than a few house names. Of course, I was not aware of the development of those Carlogie Road properties in the 1800s, nor of the fact that in 1889 the town was designated a Burgh with Commissioners and eventually, in 1901, with a Town Council with a Provost and Councillors. The eastern boundary of "early" Carnoustie was the Lochty Burn, and—with the opening of the railway station in 1838—the boundary extended to Arbroath Road and the Panbride parish boundary.

My week's pay was four shillings (or 20p in 2025), with no holidays. It could be a bit spooky in dark winter months, and growling dogs were a worry—as were freezing winds. Sleet or snow added to the hostile elements. However, there was joy over the weeks of observing the earliest crack of dawn develop into bright sunny mornings, with the birds chirping. And, of course, I "stole" a few moments to be up-to-date with news headlines. The twice-yearly change of clock-times heralded either joy or gloom.

Later, Harry also offered me an evening round to deliver *Evening Telegraph*s around a similar area as my morning round, but also including Lochty Street, Maule Street, and Philip Street. It was on Maule Street where my heart pumped greatest, for in the distance I could see Jenny Black (daughter of Jack Black the Butcher)—a lovely girl in my class at school—waiting for me to deliver the *Evening Telegraph*. I couldn't get there quickly enough. Nearly 50 years later, when she attended our school reunion (which I had arranged in 2005), I mentioned to her how she wore a bright red polo neck sweater and how

I had rushed to deliver the newspaper. To my chagrin, she had no memory of her polo-neck jumper, the paper I delivered, or—even worse—not even me! My "Adrian Mole" moments were so alive and vivid, I had held on to them for many years until that heartbreaking moment in 2005.

On a special treat day out with Harry Christie. From L to R: Norma Mirrey, James (Peem) Murray, Mr Harry Christie, and Robbie Murray.

Newspaper delivering was a tough regime, but Harry and his wife treated Peem and me—along with the only other "paperboy," who was actually a girl called Norma Mirrey (who delivered to the west end of town)—to an annual trip away in their car. I always recall that our first trip was to Braemar via the notorious Devil's Elbow. That was in the days when cars had to go down to bottom gear to make the severe turn in the road and maintain the "revs" and pace while worrying about the expectation of the car radiator boiling over! Our second annual car trip was to Pitlochry, and I recall we stopped at Dunkeld where we were treated to ice cream and strawberries in the outdoor rose garden (at the left-hand side of the road immediately before crossing the road bridge over the river Tay). Then on to Pitlochry Dam, where Harry parked his car beside the steep sloping grassy sides of the walkway. What lovely days out we had thanks to the caring boss and his wife.

When I started my message bike job with William Low & Co in 1953, I had to stop my paper round, and I was quite sorry to leave as Harry and his wife had always been so good to me.

"I still like to think my paper round sharpened me up for school each morning!"

A Message Laddie with Willie Lows

"Dinna leave the lights switched on on the message bike!"

Jim Ritchie was one of our boyhood fishing and boating "gang" at Westhaven, along with Peem, Billy Coffin and Ollie Scott. Jim worked as a delivery boy for the Co-op butchery department. One day he asked me if I'd like his butchery delivery job when he left school at the end of June 1953. The pay was to be 7/6d per week, plus a pound of mince—delivering cuts of meat, mince and potted hough. There would be no work in the shop except brushing up sawdust on the floor.

This was extremely important, because my mum was not happy about me going to work in the shop as Alec Wilmott, an apprentice, had lost an arm in the mincing machine. Mum was dead against it, but luckily Jim—being a real pal—came back to me and said that Freddie Horne was leaving William Low & Co.'s message laddie job, which paid 13/6d per week. He asked if I was interested. This solved my mum's mincing machine worry and, although it was a bigger bike with heavier loads, the pay was better. It's amazing to think that Alec Wilmott's dreadful accident and Jim Ritchie's thoughtfulness put me on my lifetime work in the grocery trade. Strangely, it had a positive impact on Alec Wilmott's life too, as he went on to become a highly respected Champion one-armed golfer.

It was July 1953, the year of Queen Elizabeth's coronation, and the summer when Ben Hogan—the American star golfer—won The Open at Carnoustie. I commenced my job with Willie Lows starting at 4 pm each day (except half-day Tuesday and all-day Saturday). Each day's work varied. Mondays were very quiet, sometimes with only one tiny delivery to Miss Barrie at The Willows—a large house at the end of Collier Street near Terrace Road. I still recall the weekly order: "three pounds of plain flour and two nutmegs." (Did no other grocer sell nutmegs?)

In addition to delivering groceries, the ladies on the staff (Cathie Reid, Isobel Kennedy, and Maggie Smith) used to ask me occasionally to do shopping chores such as hand in shoes to be re-soled or heeled, collecting shopping items, etc. I remember a shoe repairer named Leon Buller in School Road (Links Avenue), near where the Scout hut is today. I think the gentleman was German or Polish, and his workshop was a fantastic place to stop and stare whilst in his repair premises. He seemed always to have a brilliant, well-stacked coal fire burning in a large grate. He was a true craftsman, and I still recall the unique smell of freshly-cut leather and glue warmed by his spectacular fire. Later, I remember Mr D'Annunzio had a similar shoe repair business in "Fishy Lane," which ran between Kinloch Street and Dundee Street with entry next to Sutton's newspaper shop and Mr and Mrs Wallace's fruit and veg shop at No.51 Dundee Street. Sadly, Fishy Lane, (so-called because a fish shop existed there) disappeared when the Kinloch Care Centre was built in the 1990s.

Nowadays, Willie Low's shop at No.4 Dundee Street has become Boots the Chemists, but the third window nearest the old police station (the "Auld Nick") was a separate baker's shop called Keiller's, and the small window was where Keiller's door was located. That shop was Carnoustie's second Post Office.

Willie Low's business continually grew, and my territory expanded to include deliveries to Mrs Clark in the white cottage at the cross roads on the way to Panbride, to her son Miller at Parton Ha' (the cottage over the railway line at the mouth of the Craigmill Burn), and to Miss Jennings—the manager at the Soldiers' Home at Barry Buddon Camp, where I delivered large quantities of bacon and eggs.

On Saturdays I had a delivery to Cathie Reid's mum at Muirdrum; a gentle lady (and a 2/6d tip), then and another half-crown tip when I delivered to Mr Bethel (Jack Bethel's father) at the former stagecoach inn at Travebank, located at the bend where the Barry Burn flows under a bridge on the Dundee/Arbroath main road—now bypassed by the dual carriageway. Both deliveries necessitated a filled basket, and the tips were well-earned—especially when I had to get off and push the bike up the steep hill at Batty's Den on the way to Muirdrum.

After my message laddie days, I became an apprentice.
From L to R: Ian Stewart (Manager), John Thomson (Assistant Manager), Alan Longmuir (Trainee Manager), Margaret Smith, Robbie Murray, Isobel Kennedy, Cathie Reid, Kenny Leiper (Message Boy).

I learned a huge amount about other shop duties back then—sweeping floors, tidying rubbish, and putting the shop's canvas shades up and down. The boss, Mr Stewart, was very fair but he didn't like spending money on batteries for the lamps on the bike—and once the last peep of light flickered out, I had to pluck up courage to ask for money to buy new batteries at Willie Clark's cycle shop near the foot of Queen Street. Willie was a helpful man of small stature, and his nickname was "Spuggy" (a sparrow in Scotland is a Spuggy!). Sometimes the lady manager in Keiller's would ask me to put up or let down her shop's shade. I was very happy to help… but I never got a free cake!

My most nerve-wracking delivery was to the Anderson Grice foundry canteen each Monday morning. This usually consisted of bacon, eggs, sugar, tea, butter, and lard. The problem for me was that the shop didn't open till 8:30 am, and the order had to be assembled by Isobel and Cathie. In those days, sugar was sold "loose," so one pound bags of sugar had to be made up and butter "patted" into shape then wrapped in paper, all resulting in time ticking away. I was always in a panic, as I had to load up, deliver to the canteen at the far end of Taymouth Terrace, and return the message bike to the shop all before the school bell rang at 9 am. A dramatic thirty minute period! Sometimes, it would be 8.45 am or a minute or two later before I set off, so I was "creasing myself" on the return journey only to hear the school bell being rung and lines being formed in the playground as I pedalled past, knowing I still had to park the message bike then cycle my way to school. Amazingly, there always seemed to be a "magic minute" or two while pupils in front of me went to the cloakroom before getting into class. Phew! By some miracle I never got the "belt" for being late, and I don't think the boss and staff ever knew how close I was to that terror. A strong wind in either direction could have resulted in me suffering the "Lochgelly tawse" (that is, the dreaded strap!).

I eventually advanced from my days as a message laddie, and all that (and more) is contained in my *Grocer's Boy* trilogy (2018–22).

"I learned so much about life being a message boy at Willie Lows!"

Radio and TV Apprenticeship

"The fowk at the fit o' the toon buy the most expensive sets!"

By 1955, I knew the message bike job very well, and I was due to leave school at the tattie holidays (my 15th birthday being on the 22nd October). My pal Willie Yool had started work as a joinery apprentice with Edward and Ramsay (off Ferrier Street), and although I greatly enjoyed technical subjects and "techy drawing," I was keen to do something different. Alan Craigie (son of Craigie's

Bakery—today, a shop operated by J.M. Bakery) was a radio and TV apprentice with Ron Soutar (where Crazy Cuts hairdresser is located in 2025). This was the new world of TV engineering, and it seemed like a good job for the future. By chance, I saw an advert in the *Guide and Gazette* for a radio and TV engineering apprentice with Reekie's of Arbroath.

At the end of October, I started my apprenticeship with Reekie on a weekly pay of £1-10/- (£1.50). My message boy pay had been 13/6d per week, and with substantial tips which had provided me with more than my radio apprenticeship weekly wage. My tasks were mundane. I filled acid batteries and put them on charge. I kept the workshop floor tidy and tended the coal fire in the workshop, as well as regularly unpacking and preparing new TV sets by putting on a plug ready for an engineer to test them before delivery.

Senior engineers at the company were Jim Kennedy, Davie Milne, and Ernie Small. Bob Cruickshank was a nineteen-year-old 3rd year apprentice, and it was with him that I spent most of my time travelling around the town and a large part of the countryside in a Reekie van which Bob drove furiously. He loved driving (and I feared an early death), but I began to build up a knowledge of the town and country villages. We were kept busy collecting radios and television sets for repair, as well as delivering and setting up repaired and new sets. Bob had a mattress on the floor of the van on which TV sets were safely transported.

Radios and television sets functioned with a wide range of components, including valves, resisters, condensers, and transformers, and joints were soldered. Sets sat on a ten-foot-long workbench for days, and often weeks, while engineers tried to fathom out the cause of a malfunction. The "insides" of a set were pulled out of their containers and were surrounded by a mass of wires, nuts, bolts, screws and washers. How everything went back into its proper place I'll never know—and I think then, deep down, I didn't want to know. Inside a six-foot-high wall cabinet, all components were stored, and the nearest I got to helping was—on request—to pass a component over to a mechanic. All component items had a reference, and I recall handing over items such as an "EY161 valve" or a "341 R resistor." I didn't get as far as understanding what they did—they were simply numbers to me.

Television sets came with familiar names such as Pye, Echo, and Ferranti. Some were table models or consoles—the latter being a TV inside a tall four or five-foot-tall, floor-standing cabinet with doors. Some had high-quality wood veneer, and choices were available such as walnut, mahogany, etc. Consoles were more expensive, and it was mainly fisher families at the "fit o' the toon" and farmers who were able to afford them.

Davie Milne was a very helpful man, and took me to the harbour where he was an expert on boats' echo-sounders and radios. My heart leapt at the thought of learning about boats' equipment, but one day he dismayed me by saying I wouldn't get on board because of my red hair. There were fishers' superstitions that red hair was not welcome—I learned later that this was because of the Vikings.

Effectively the Vikings' 700-year-old history had ended any hopes I had of learning about boats' radios.

By starting in October, I was too late to begin year one of the engineering day release classes at Dundee Technical College, which meant I would be 16 years old before I could start my studies. Effectively, my years as an apprentice were also delayed, and the prospect of earning a decent wage seemed a long way off. Combined with the mundane tasks and the Vikings' intervention, I eventually lost interest. What I discovered was not only these negatives, but also the fact that I missed the vibrancy and pace of working in Willie Lows.

One evening, in Spring 1956, on impulse I propped my bicycle against the kerb outside the shop at No.4 Dundee Street and asked my old boss if I could start an apprenticeship in the grocery trade. After an agonising one week wait, it was confirmed I could start my apprenticeship. Like Jim's offer of a message bike job, it was to be a key moment in my working life.

The job of a radio and TV engineer didn't last long, as circuit boards soon replaced them. As the old adage goes, "food, clothing, and shelter are the essentials of life."

"In retrospect, I learned early in life that I was a 'people person'."

Not our car! From L to R:
Tom Nicol, Robbie Murray, Bill McGregor,
David Yool, Rich Simmons.

CHAPTER 7

Motoring

Motorbike Days

"I knew while wearing my dad's old railway coat and my 'egg top' crash helmet that I was no James Dean!"

Today, in 2025, there are a few motorbikes around, and in many cases it's mature men who enjoy reliving the motorbike experience. When I was 17 years old, there were many young guys around who owned a motorbike. It seemed it was the obvious progression from a push-bike. Perhaps it was the simple fact that I, like my pals, liked the feeling of independence.

On my Tuesdays' half-day off, while employed in the Carnoustie branch of Wm Low & Co., I frequented Dundee city centre shops in the afternoon prior to attending my usual Grocers' Institute night class at Commercial College in Cowgate, Dundee. A motorcycle shop in the Overgate was always a magnet for me to stroll around and gaze at the wide range of bikes for sale. The smell of petrol, oil and exhausts was mesmeric to me.

As a "lightweight" lad, I was never going to be able to handle something powerful, and I started looking at B.S.A. Bantams (100 or 150 cc), but that didn't appeal. The B.S.A. 250 cc was an obvious choice, but that was an expensive option at around £150/£250. The price of an older, heavy bike was more acceptable, but a heavy bike needing work carried out was not an attractive idea.

Eventually I settled on a £69 Triumph 3T—that was a 350 cc machine (in reality a silly decision), with twin exhausts and an ex-Army telescopic stand which removed the need to pull it up on its stand every time I parked. All I then needed was my own kit. I bought a crash helmet (not compulsory equipment back then) which resembled the decapitated top of an egg, and my jacket was my dad's redundant thick black British Rail coat. My goggles were of the "Biggles" type—which, in retrospect, must have been picked up in a second-hand sale somewhere. When I looked in the mirror, I knew I was no James Dean!

How I first drove my motor bike from the showroom in the centre of Dundee to Carnoustie I'll never know. It served me well, though—I drove to Saturday evening dances with my motor bike friends to places like Kirriemuir, Brechin, and Arbroath. In theory,

Robbie models his motorbike in the garden of No.4 Shamrock Street, Carnoustie.

the "bike" meant that if I wanted to walk a girl home and be independent, there was no rush for a bus. In addition to motorbiking to dances, my pals and I could have runs into the country on Sunday afternoons, or I could drive around on my half-days off.

A turning point came when I passed my motorbike driving test. This was quite an experience. Of course, I had swotted the Highway Code and so applied to sit my test.

I was mystified as to how the test would be carried out, but I soon discovered. The driving test took place, as planned, in Arbroath. The examiner explained that I should drive around in a circuit, doing left-turns around blocks of houses. I set off and wondered how things would develop. I soon found out, for he suddenly appeared in the road and waved me down. The next instruction was to turn around and complete the circuit doing right-hand turns. He reappeared and then required me to do a "figure eight" around two different blocks of houses. I remember having to concentrate exactly where I was and, at one point, I thought I'd lost him—until, without any warning, he suddenly leapt out from behind some parked cars, causing me to slam on the brakes. Of course, I then realised that was how he conducted the "emergency stop" test.

All went well, and I happily returned to Carnoustie and took the "L-plates" off. Then, with a big smile, I cruised up Shamrock Street so mum would immediately spot my success. Quite soon after my "pass," I was able to help my father in a practical way. He had to get to Lunan Bay signal box for 6.30 am and, as his moped was out of action, I drove him on my pillion seat. Having a pillion passenger scared me, and I can only imagine how petrified my poor father must have been.

The greatest speed I ever reached on my bike was 82 m.p.h. Well, to be honest, it was a nudge over 80 on my speedometer. This breakneck speed was achieved on a long straight on the road to Forfar, where at one point (it has gone now) there was a humpback bridge. This had the effect of lifting my bum off the seat and, for a few seconds, causing me to have contact with my bike only via the handlebars. It was exhilarating—with the added fear that I had to brake hard immediately after landing back on the seat to safely negotiate a sharp left-hand bend. I dared not tell mum I did such stupid things.

My greatest shock came when, on the long straight road between Arbroath and Brechin—just beyond the Kinnell crossroads—I stopped to adjust my goggles and to do so put down the telescopic stand. Once on the road again and approaching a dip and a left-hand bend, I started to lean the bike over, but for some strange reason it wouldn't tip. I looked down and, to my horror, saw flying sparks. I immediately realised they were caused by the base of my stand (still expanded), which was scraping the roadway. There was no way at speed I could bend backwards in my seat and pull the wire to release the stand, so I had to start braking and keep going in a straight line—which meant driving on the wrong side of the road. Praying that nothing would come towards me, I gradually brought the speed down, but just when I felt I was safe a car came round the bend facing me. Luckily the driver could brake faster than me, but we each ended up stationary—staring at each other. I got off my bike, rested it on the stand, and walked to explain and apologise to the startled driver. I'm lucky still to be around to smile every time I pass that spot!

One other memorable moment was my visit to dancing at Kirriemuir. It was a dreadful night of wind and rain, and when I reached the dance hall I paid my entrance money but soon realised I was so wet I couldn't sit down.

I had to spend all evening drying myself and belongings on a radiator. Not a single dance, no girl to take home and a wet seat on the bike when I stepped out to drive back to Carnoustie. Ah well—it seemed like a good idea at the time!

It's amazing what tales come back to me. I remember on a wet day on cassies (cobbles) and tram lines, driving up Lochee Road in Dundee when the bike simply slid out from below me. Gently, yet nightmarishly, the bike and me seemed to glide along the road and end up at a bus stop with a queue of ladies. "Are you alright, son?" is all I remember one startled lady ask. That was at the right-hand bend, with a big church on the left-hand side of the road—just near the start of Logie Street. Today I smile as I pass that spot, too!

Of course, my biggest smile of relief, still to this day, is when I escaped from an accident at the first of the two sharp bends on the way towards Muirdrum one Sunday evening in 1957. I was turning right on the first bend when a car, driven by a learner on the wrong side of the road, on their way towards

The car on the wrong side of the road, displaying an L-plate and my bike wrecked. David Yool, who was following me, looks on.

"Paddy's Mansion," knocked me off my bike. This resulted in me landing on the verge and sustaining a broken wrist. No mobile phones with cameras in those days, otherwise the position of the car would have been conclusive evidence. No-one was charged, but the part that still upsets me is that it always, then, seemed to be that the motorcyclist was in the wrong or was supposedly driving too fast—or both!

However, a press photograph from the time tells the real story.

When fit enough, I visited Strachan's Garage in the High Street to inspect my bike, only to find it in an ugly, sad state with the handlebars folded up as if by a giant. The insurance company told me I had no claim, as the frame—on inspection—revealed it had been previously in an accident and was not roadworthy. I probably could have argued, but wherever possible insurance companies always try to find a reason or excuse not to pay out.

Despite the injustice, I am lucky to be alive to smile as I drive past that spot. Three motorbiking friends of mine were killed on bikes around that period—and none were at fault. A classmate, Sandy McAuley, was travelling towards the town on the stretch of road between Bleachfield and Westhaven Farm. A car was reversing out of the farm area on the north side of the road, and Sandy had no time to break. Roddy Black was riding on the pillion of a bike which somehow left the road and caused him to be thrown against a tree. Roddy had a serious injury to his back. I remember we, as the Church Bible class, went to sing Christmas carols at his bedside in Arbroath Infirmary. We were all concerned about Roddy, who maintained a smiling face, but several weeks later he died of his injuries.

The story of Bill Bisset's death was sadly another tragedy. He was driving along Dundee Street towards the Corner Hotel late one night (or very early Sunday morning) with, evidently, no other traffic around when he hit a kerb-side lamppost outside the bungalow at No.136 Dundee Street opposite The Stag's Head pub. It seems his windshield was struck by a bird, and that was enough to distract him—he lost control. A news reporter at the time said a dead starling was found lying beside his bike. Another theory was that he hit a flock of seagulls which were picking up fish and chip scraps off the road at that point. I witnessed some of the bike debris when I delivered newspapers to the bungalow that Sunday morning. It was after this accident that lamp posts in the town were gradually removed from kerb-side positions.

"Statistically, I'm lucky to be alive!"

Cars

"I'll keep your golf clubs until you pay all instalments!"

With my motorbike scrapped, I had no temporary means of travelling to the usual Saturday dances. I was lucky to discover that Bill Campbell of West Smieton Street had organised a bus to go to wherever Saturday evening public dances were planned in Angus towns. The bus left from Barry Road at the top of Victoria Street at about 7 pm, so for me it was a quick dash home when the shop closed at 6 o'clock. This was probably the safest and least expensive way to travel in comfort with no worries.

Much to my mum's comfort, my biking days were at an end. The untimely deaths of my friends, regular soakings on the way to dances, and the danger of icy roads had taken the "shine" off the thrill of motor biking. It seemed a better idea to get a car.

Around this time, one of my friends—who didn't have a bike, and was working with the Co-op—came to the rescue. Tom Nicol (twin brother of Jim) was at that time able to give me a brief but illegal opportunity to drive the Co-op milk van (sorry, Tom—I did promise never to tell anyone) along the grassy strip between the lines of Buckie Hillocks' holiday huts on the seaside of the railway line near Westhaven farm. This was enough to give me the feel of driving a vehicle, and my hunt for a car was on.

Tom and I checked the "cars for sale" in *The Courier* newspaper, and eventually found a Wolseley 14 on offer at £27.10/- from a man in Glamis. We subsequently viewed it, and found it to be a black limousine, the same type that featured in the BBC TV programme *Z-Cars*. The smell of real leather and the space inside was impressive. Somehow, we must have been given a lift to Glamis, for Tom accompanied me as I drove it back to Carnoustie under my provisional car licence. Along with it came lots of spares which I never used but which—unfortunately, to my father's annoyance—took up valuable space in his shed.

It was an immediate "hit" with my pals, for we could now (with a qualified driver beside me) get to dances in one vehicle—yes, all five or six of us at at time, with not a seatbelt in sight. Petrol costs were shared, and we had some adventures on the way—the scariest one being on our journey home one Saturday night, when we came to the high ground between Forfar and Carnoustie and discovered the visibility due to hill mist was down to only a few yards. With many bends in the road and roadside ditches, it was risky. Tom, who was sitting in the front with me, said, "Stop the car, Robbie! I have an idea." He then stepped outside, wound down the window, closed the door, and stood on the exterior running board. Problem solved—Tom gave me directions about my distance from the grass verges as I drove at a slow, safe speed. I didn't dare think how close Tom came to ending up in a ditch.

One day, as I stood filling the petrol tank—or should I say, putting in a gallon and a half—I glanced down at a rear wheel and noticed that a wheel nut was loose. No other nuts appeared slack, so I drove home and checked all of the nuts, only to find that while the wheel drum bolts were steel, the nuts were brass—and more alarmingly, that the threads on some brass nuts were badly worn. Recollecting a science lesson about the relative strengths or durability of metals, I knew this could not be good news. I sold the car immediately for £32. 10/-. Amazingly, this was a profit—and I felt obliged to tell the buyer about the wheel nuts.

The car had served me well, and my friends and I had enjoyed our dancing adventures to and from venues all over Angus. Still to the present day, I tell the embarrassing story of how I made that profit when I sold the Wolseley. I had advertised it in the local *Guide and Gazette*, and a prospective buyer—who lived in Victoria Street—contacted me. The man, quite a bit older than myself, said he couldn't pay outright but asked if he could pay me by postal order at 10 shillings(50p) a month. I was not too sure about this, but recalled from my evening classes the concept of "collateral." I suggested to the buyer that I needed some security while he paid the instalments. We agreed that I would keep his golf clubs until the total sum was paid. All went well but, along with his last instalment, there was a note requesting me to now send on his clubs! When the discussions had started, he was living in Carnoustie, and he was a Carnoustie person. Thus I wrongly assumed he would be back for his clubs. Alas, I had to pay a delivery fee to have them sent by rail to Thurso, where he now lived! My handsome profit was badly damaged. I learned an expensive lesson that day.

My Wolseley had been far too big a car to keep on the road, but it had provided me with a training period to get used to roads and driving. After six lessons with a driving instructor, I applied to sit my test and passed in his car, driving around the blocks of houses in Arbroath where I had passed my motorbike test only a year earlier. My silly, short period of dashing about on a motorbike and a "too big" car were now over. My next car would be a Ford Prefect 1954 model, which I purchased from Alex Reid's garage in Dundee Street in 1960.

"But I could never have been a Stirling Moss!"

Petrol

"One and a half gallons please, and a squirt of Redex!"

Out for a wet Sunday afternoon walk on a muddy, unmade Church Street pavement in 1950. In the background, Dave Fyfe's garage and filling station. From L to R: Dad, Jean Fyfe's St Bernard dog, Peem, Robbie, and Isobel.

Today, in 2025, the town does not offer a petrol or diesel filling station. In the 1950s there were several fuel stations. No diesel back then, of course—only petrol and engine oil were available. There was a pump located at the Post Office shop near the bridge in Barry village. On Barry Road, Carnoustie, near the Corner Hotel (now a Co-op food store), there were a few pumps. Esso fuel was available, followed by Burmah which closed in the 1980s. Thereafter, the nearest filling stations are in Arbroath.

Ramsay the joiners, located on the east side of the small north section of Brown Street, also offered a single petrol pump, while Alex Reid had a few pumps at his garage at No.148 Dundee Street. Strachan's (later Fairways) garage in Dundee Street (the art deco building near the top of Fox Street) offered the best range of graded petrol. Upstairs in that building were two privately-occupied homes which still, as of 2025, are occupied. The previous large garage workshop area is now a car park, and in the old forecourt area as well as in the general parking area are electric car battery charge points. The ambulance was based at Strachan's, and the regular driver was Mr Bob McDiarmid. Mr Drummond was also a driver, and he and his family occupied one of the flats upstairs. Strachan's, during the summers of the 1950s and '60s, offered a range of one-day bus trips to popular places such as Beech Hedges, Pitlochry, Reekie-linn, Glen Esk, and Aberfeldy. An array of display boards depicting views of each venue were cleverly drawn in coloured chalk, on boards, to help advertise each trip.

My usual refill spot was at Dave Fyfe's small premises, where he offered petrol and Redex at a pump located on the blaize pavement at the door of his motorcar workshop on the south side of Church Street. He extended his filling station later. But was a spot of Redex reckoned to give added power, or better m.p.g.?

"A motorbike, petrol, and a sunny day offered freedom and independence!"

CHAPTER 8
A Few More Thoughts

Some Scots Words and Phrases o' My Day

"Baffies and Breeks"

When I grew up as a boy, I ran around using everyday Scottish words and phrases. Gradually, between schooling and my work environment, I began to "speak properly." Added to changes in my life and work, there was also the influence of "BBC English" which was purported—by some—to be "the right way to speak."

In my case, both parents were from farming families—my mother's parents worked all their days "on the land" and, in the case of my dad's background, his own father started work as a farm labourer and moved on to work on the railways (L.M.S.), becoming a signalman, while his wife was from an engineering 'smiddy' family.

Consequently, I grew up with Scottish words and terms at home and in the school playground. In time, I came to discover that mum was actually "bi-lingual"—using her native language, but adopting "correct" English when speaking with, for example, doctors, ministers, and some shopkeepers. I also found myself similarly adjusting my own language when I spoke with my customers in the retail grocery trade. Later, in my managerial life as I moved about the UK on business, I spoke the Queen's English exclusively (except perhaps for the occasional Anglo-Saxon word I may have employed whilst driving in London!).

However, I still revert to old Scottish words and phrases when telling jokes and stories: they should not be allowed to die. Some phrases from my early life I recall, and which I never hear nowadays, are noted below:

"A skelp on the lug." ("A slap on your ear.")

"A scone on the lug." (As above.)

"A sicht fur sair een." (A sight for sore eyes.)

"What a sicht!" (A derogatory remark—"What a sight!")

"Ach, no afore yer tea!" ("Please don't eat too much before your evening meal.")

"Dinna say things like that." ("Don't speak like that.")

"Harken tae that!" ("Listen to that!" Exclaimed with a degree of surprise or incredulity.)

"Ants in your pants." (Someone who fidgets or moves about a lot.)

"Yer like a flea on a blanket!" or "Yer like a hen on a hot griddle." (To someone who jumps about nervously. A griddle was a cooking tray.)

"Come in aboot." ("Gather around me.")

"Awa' ye go!" ("Go away," or "Don't be silly.")

"Dinna speir ower much!" ("Don't ask too many questions.")

"Aye, ah ken!" ("Yes, I know!")

"Tak' care; guid fowk are scarce." (Said on departing: "Take care—good people are hard to find.")

"Haste ye back." (Said on departing: "Come and visit again soon.")

"Dinna squeeze that plook!" ("Don't squeeze that pimple!")

"Pit oan your cosy baffies!" ("Put on your warm slippers.")

"Pit on your new breeks!" ("Put on your new trousers.")

"Ca' canny!" ("Take your time," or "Take great care.")

"Dinna be sae dozent!" ("Don't be so stupid.")

"Yer up afore yer claes are on!" ("You're up earlier this morning!")

"Skin the rabbit!" (A joke while changing very tight clothes on a young child.)

"Yer feet are a' weet!" ("Your feet are all wet!")

"Watch ye dinna cowp yer cert!" ("Take care not to overturn your cart (barrow)!")

"Aye, there's a fine drooth the day!" ("Yes, it's a nice drying day today!"—referring to clothes on the washing line.)

"That's a muckle load ye ha'e there!" ("That is a very big load you have there!")

"That's a richt balder ye got the day!" ("That is quite a serious short haircut you got today!")

"Jist pit they things ben the hoose!" ("Please put those items through to another room.")

"Ca' yer gird!" ("Get moving faster!"—a gird was an iron hoop, about 24 or 30 inches in diameter and with a half-inch depth which was made to roll along a road by means of a metal rod with a hook on the end.)

"Aye he's lookin' a bit haiket the day!" ("Yes, he is looking rather untidy today!")

"Dinna pit aff!" ("Don't waste time in your endeavours!")

"Gie it a dicht!" ("Give it a wipe with a cloth!")

"Aye, yer gi sweered to get up the day." ("Yes, you are rather reluctant get out of bed today.")

"Come in a' hent." ("Move in behind me.")

"That's a fair sooch o' a wind!" ("That's quite a strong wind.")

"Now mind and change yer semmit the day!" ("Remember to put on a clean/fresh vest today.")

"Watch oot; yer shoppie door's open!" ("Take care, your flies are unbuttoned.")

"You'll have travel by Shank's Pony." ("You will have to walk there.")

"What a fleg you ge'ed me!" ("What a scare you gave me!")

"Dinna mak' a sclerry wi' that!" ("Please don't make a mess of that!")

"Dicht yersel' doon." ("Dust yourself down.")

Do you Remember the Wee Things?

"Attention now, Murray and Blair—you're on milk duty this week!"

While writing this peek into my "good old days" in Carnoustie, and my family experiences which I was so fortunate to enjoy, it is the multitude of "wee things" that have remained with me all my life, and I feel the need to include them in this look.

My attempt to capture a bygone age leads me to include so many of my unforgettable memories. Where to start is my first question, and so I have decided to mention the "wee things" in some sort of order, such as those encountered during school life.

School Life

"Attention now, Murray and Blair—it's your turn to carry in the milk crate this week!" said Mr McHutcheon (Hutchie), the 11+ "Quali-teacher." (Each week, two boys were designated to collect and carry in the crate of milk bottles for the class.)

Some of the wee things:

- The thin cardboard cap (with perforated space for a straw) on our free bottle of milk (one third of a pint), and damaging the straw when trying to pierce it.

- My school bag containing a small bottle of water, along with a piece of cloth which I used to clean my slate board each day.

- Each desk inkwell, being re-filled by a designated pupil using a large bottle of ink.

- Slides on the icy playground.

- Male pupils fighting for a chance to ring the school bell at the end of playtime and lunchtime.

- The wooden pencil-case carried inside my school-bag.

- Coloured raffia in long strands, used in handiwork classes hanging on the back of a cupboard door in Miss Murray's classroom.

- Examination questions written on a swivel blackboard which would be turned over to reveal questions when the exam started, or a roller-board would be 'revolved' to reveal the dreaded questions.

- Girls going home with the cooked meals they had produced in their "domestic class."

- Subjects up to the 11+ year included reading, grammar, arithmetic, and writing, which we referred to as "compositions" (essays). In the 11+ year, we were "sharpened up" each morning with a rapid burst of ten mental arithmetic questions.

Footwear

"I've put new tackets on the heels of your boot, so don't go making sparks on the roads!"

- Boots: These were worn in winter. Dad, using his shoemaker's last (a form, shaped like a foot, used to manufacture and repair footwear), hammered in "tackets" around the edge of the heels and stuck on rubber soles. Not good for "slides" in the playground, but great for making sparks on the road or pavement!

- Sandals: Once the winter boots were put aside, we wore sandals from May to the end of September. As we grew, we were given new sandals each spring, and the old ones (with the toes cut out) were used to wear when we ran about on the beach and rocks.

- Sandshoes: We required sandshoes for gym at school and they, like the sandals, were upgraded each year.

- Socks: As youngsters, we wore only long socks. Holes in heels were repaired by mum's darning. We needed garters to keep our socks up.

Clothing

"You're not going out to play until you change your clothes!" mum ordered.

We had very definite "school wear," but when we were at home or out playing we had "playwear"—plus, of course, our "Sunday best" wear. We were brought up to look after our clothing carefully. While at Admiral Street, Peem and I shared a bed in the smaller bedroom, and a large trunk where we carefully stored our clothing. When I was given my first pair of long trousers, I pressed them overnight under my mattress. Wintertime saw us wearing a warm jacket and a wool balaclava.

Personal Washing

"Wash your hands before you go any further!"

With an occasional bath in the washhouse, all we needed was to daily wash our face and hands (and knees!) at the kitchen sink. We were instructed to clean our teeth daily, and I recall in those days we had no toothpaste tubes but instead used a communal small, flat, round tin of toothpaste.

Homework

"You're not getting out to play until you do your homework!"

As soon as the evening meal was over, the dining table was cleared and each of us had a side of the table where we could write our homework. Usually, we wrote pieces in pencil, and then used a pen and ink to do a final copy. As we progressed, we had more subjects to study and were strictly controlled to do our homework and be in bed by 8.15 pm. Some evenings we were allowed to listen to special radio programmes up to as late as 8.45 pm or 9 pm. Our radio was one with a high-powered dry battery which had to be replaced every so often. *Dick Barton: Special Agent* came on about 9 pm, but sadly we were chased off to bed before it started. On Sunday lunchtimes we listened to *Billy Cotton's Band Show*, and—in the evenings—*The Ovaltinies*. I also recall a radio comedy show called *The McFlannels*, which I think was broadcast on a Saturday evening.

Television

"That's three TV aerials up in Shamrock Street now!"

It was 1956–57 when we acquired our first rental TV set. It had a black and white screen, of course. Daily, the last broadcast was at around 10 pm, when the national anthem played and the last light spot disappeared off the screen. There was a point in time when it was fun to count the growing number of TV aerials being fitted on rooftops.

It wasn't until the 1980s and I was married with two children that I bought a colour TV and enjoyed late evening TV programmes.

Indoor Games

With few suitable radio programmes for children (except *The Ovaltinies*), we spent time playing ludo, tiddly-winks, draughts, snakes and ladders, and snap. Handiwork such as catty-tails, raffia mats, and possibly some embroidery, also took place. All in all, those cosy winter evenings with a glorious roasting fire were heavenly. Peace, quiet, energy, excitement, and good fun. Then off to bed with a "piggy" hot water bottle—not a lot of money. Two "piggy bottles" (a glazed earthenware container) were not allowed into your bed unless they were wrapped up. That was mum's strict rule. Why? Because of the danger of them cracking. But what great expense and luxury having TWO of them!

I'm certain mum and dad scraped every penny to look after us. In contrast to those cosy evenings was the Jack Frost—fern pattern icy designs on the inside of the window. Then a jolt into reality, especially when our bare feet touched the cold linoleum flooring. We were not harshly disciplined—it was, I think, our unwitting learning of witnessing our parents care, attention and economic use of limited funds that made us realise the need to "behave" ourselves.

Interests

While girls were probably baking cakes with mum or playing with prams and dollies, boys spent time making bows and arrows, catapults, or fishing rods, or were running around playing cowboys and Indians firing at each other with cap-guns. (These were toy guns which made a "crack" when the trigger was pulled.) Model boats and yachts were popular ideas, and so too was the pastime of making our bikes sound like motorcars by fastening stiff cardboard on to the frame so that the wheel spokes created an engine noise.

We must have driven locals wild by doing "time trials" around the square—i.e. Admiral Street, Tayside Street, Norries Road, and Mariner Street. We loved the thrill of imagining we were on motorbikes but dad was not amused as he said it was slackening our spokes! We did, however, look after our bicycles very well with regular oiling, checking our lamp batteries, repairing tyres, and (if we had one) making sure our dynamo was working. Maintenance was critical, otherwise we would face spending our pocket money on an essential item.

We enjoyed the changes the seasons brought—long, clear nights as spring emerged, when we could play outside until bedtime, followed by the gathering early dark cold evenings as winter approached. There was a cosy pattern to our life. Street games occupied us in many ways. There were a few favourites: walking on stilts, skipping (with variations including high, low, medium, dolly, rocky, pepper), and hopscotch—or "Plallies," as we termed it. Another street game, but not a nice one, was "chickie-mellie." This entailed knocking on doors (or ringing doorbells) and running away. An added thrill was to hide behind something and watch the perplexed householder standing there looking puzzled. Anti-social behaviour!

When I was about eleven or twelve years old, I used to cycle with my pal John Robb (who lived in Ireland Street) to the High Road—sometimes called the Dundee/Arbroath Toll Road—where we sat for hours in the long grass on the north side of the road where the road from Clayholes joined the High Road. Once settled, we got out our jotters (notebooks) and wrote down the registration of every vehicle that passed by. In those days, the vehicles had a number relating to the local tax office where the vehicle was registered. The AA (Automobile Association) published a list of what the registration letters on the number plate meant. E.g. YJ was a Dundee registration, and SR was Angus. I think we simply wanted to know where vehicles had come from, and we did find some very unusual places.

Other games I played were along with Peem and Coffie, when we explored the Barry Buddon Army training ground where we played on assault course obstacles. This was a seriously silly pastime, firstly because the tests were for grown-up fit soldiers and secondly there were reports (which we knew about) that wartime mortar bombs had been used during war time training and were still lying about.

In the autumn, a favourite game was "conkers." This entailed drilling a hole through a chestnut and threading string through it. The game then was to compete with your friends in the game of "conkers," the aim of which was to find whose "conker" was the winner by destroying other weaker ones. I can honestly say there was never an idle moment. Our time as children was filled with such a variety of engaging activity.

When we reached a certain age, we played "catch and kiss." This was a game involving a few girls and boys. The girls would scatter in different directions and then hide. When found by a boy, he was "entitled" (by the rules of the game, at least) to ask her for a kiss. The sides could then be reversed when the boys would hide. It was essentially a game of "hide and seek" with a little bit of innocent young teenager fun added in.

What secrets we kept from mums and dads!

Helping at Home

I have related elsewhere my Saturday chores, when I was able to help mum with shopping for bakeries and groceries. With mum occasionally doing part-time cooking and cleaning jobs (she cleaned the Royal Bank of Scotland offices, and cooked and cleaned for Mrs Aimer at her guest house in Philip Street), there were additional Saturday duties to keep us occupied.

Setting the Fire

Cleaning out the old coal fire ashes, and resetting the fire ready for lighting later in the day, was one such duty. This entailed shovelling out the ash and depositing it in the outdoors dustbin. We used newspaper and dad's supply of kindling made from railway sleepers (which Peem and I had often helped to saw on a trestle), and gave off a unique, warmed tarry pine aroma. Small pieces of coal were then laid on the kindling, all then ready for one match to set it off. Occasionally, if my construction of the foundation of the fire was not good enough, it was necessary to hold a large sheet of newspaper over the entire front of the fireplace to "give it a blow." To this day, I can still recall the warm, wood-scented smell which developed. The crucial point, of course, was never to allow the newspaper to catch fire!

Coal

As a supplement to coal, dad produced what he called "slush." This was the coal dust saved from inside the coal bunker, mixed with water to produce a "slush" (or sludge?) which was useful to place on top of a very hot, glowing fire to dampen down the "burn" and have a longer, more economic fire. Similarly, Peem and I, along with Billy Coffin, occasionally on Saturdays went to the gasworks and stood in a queue to buy a large sack of "coke," costing two shillings and sixpence (12.5p). This was another way of prolonging a fire, but in this case the coke aided a greater and more intensely glowing fire.

"Yes, we had some real 'roasters'."

Food

Mum and dad produced most of our food by growing vegetables, making jam, and buying as much produce as possible which could be cooked or baked. Few canned or packeted items were purchased—mum made all her own soups, stews, and sweets such as custard and rice puddings. She was trained as a cook, but when I think back to the days when we were all at home she toiled tirelessly and uncomplainingly, making the most tasty and healthy meals. Mum's brother, my uncle Jim Taylor—a farm manager at Ethiebeaton farm near Monifieth—occasionally gifted us with a honeycomb from his beehives which he kept in the Angus Glens.

In days before we had a fridge, mum used a marble-top cabinet on which to store some foods. Along with this, the only other storage place was the 'meat-safe'. This was a wooden frame, made by dad, which was covered all round by very fine mesh to keep out flies and insects while allowing cold air to circulate around more perishable foods. Of course, it was limited to use only in cooler or cold days, but out of the sun even in summer it was beneficial.

Favourite treats were toffee apples which mum made by pouring melted toffee over apples on a waxed tray the homemade sticks having been inserted earlier. After cooling and when the toffee was crisp, we were allowed to select from the tray. The bonus was the flat piece of toffee where the apple had sat upside-down. Another favourite were pancakes cooked on the new flat base of mum's first electric hob. At supper time a favourite was "steepies"— that was broken rich tea biscuit pieces in warm milk. (Yes, we were truly spoiled bairns!) Mum's delicious rice puddings are also memorable. Baked in a deep tray, the aroma was mouth-watering, and the rippling roasted skin is still a wonderful memory.

Food deliveries to homes were commonplace back then. For example:

- The Co-op bread van called twice weekly. I recall seeing the driver use a very long "paddle" to pull out a loaf from deep inside the covered van.

- A coalman with horse and cart delivered, weekly, coal that was emptied straight into the coal bunker.

- Bottled milk was delivered daily to the doorstep from Clark's of Barry's milk float, which moved at great speed around the streets—with young lads hopping on and off a platform at the rear of the lorry.

- Fish ladies from Arbroath should not be forgotten. They travelled by train to Carnoustie and walked around the town dressed in traditional blue and white striped long dress outfits, delivering fish to customers' homes. Today, we have an excellent weekly supply of fresh fish from an Arbroath lady who sells from a van in the street.

From my earliest days while living at Barry Road and later at Admiral Street, we enjoyed the weekly visit of the "Sweetie Man." He came, in all weathers, from Arbroath, and he sold tea which he told mum he had packed into quarter-pound packets at his base in Arbroath. He also sold sweets and biscuits. He was an amazing man who deserved every sale he made, for he carried his stock in separate containers—large biscuit tins were hung diagonally across each shoulder, and one contained sweets while the other held biscuits. He also slung a small suitcase, containing tea, around his neck which rested on his chest. As if that wasn't enough, he carried a suitcase in each hand which contained his added stocks. He wore the same clothes in summer and winter, comprising a long raincoat, trousers, and cloth cap. He was a gentle, non-pushy, ruddy-faced, polite man, and somehow he seemed to know we had moved to Westhaven. Mum always treated us to a sweetie purchased from the man, and I suspect she bought biscuits and tea from simply because she admired his efforts.

Laundry

Gathering in washing was another regular household task. It was a great thrill to be asked by mum, especially in winter, to bring in the

The Arbroath Sweetie Man dressed the same in summer and winter. Sketch by James "Peem" Murray.

washing from the outside washing line—not least if the sheets were solidly frozen, as they had to be brought into the house upright.

In the days before paper tissues, the normal practice was to use linen handkerchiefs for nose-blowing. This was acceptable, as they would be washed along with clothing and bedding. However, if hankies were soaked by nose-blowing, mum had to boil them in a separate wash ladle. Another trick she picked up at Dunninald Castle, perhaps?

Housework

With no vacuum cleaners in our house until the late 1950s or early 1960s, we had only a brush and shovel to sweep all around the linoleum floors. I do remember using a Ewbank floor sweeper, which swept up dust by roller brushes contained in a small enclosure at the end of a brush handle. It worked best on carpets or rugs. I recall a vacuum cleaner salesman coming to the house to show us how to use it.

Spare buttons were another example of making do and mending. I recall mum's big tin container, full to the brim with every imaginable colour, size and shape of button. It was another essential part of her household kit of wonder solutions.

Health and First Aid

The last time I can recall a doctor visiting me at home was when I was around 13 years old. That was when I had camped at Panmure Estate with my fellow Scout patrol leaders and carelessly drank un-boiled water from a burn. The result was sickness and very high temperature (to say nothing of white stools!). Dr McConnell arrived mid-morning after a call to the surgery by mum from the telephone kiosk at Norrie Street in Westhaven. The days of doctors' home visits around the town began to decline from around the mid 1960s.

While speaking of health, I should add something about my dentist. He was Mr Archibald Clark, whose surgery was above the Wm Low & Co. shop (now Boots the Chemist in 2025) at No.4 Dundee Street. The dreaded drill was powered by a succession of pulleys which drove the speed of the drill bit—it seemed cumbersome and certainly compared badly with today's speedy, quieter versions. For extractions, injections were available, but he also used gas to "knock out" his patients prior to the procedure.

Enough said about doctors and dentists. In my early years, I was never aware of people being trained as "first-aiders" (or first responders, as we use the term nowadays) unless perhaps a soldier or a Boy Scout had been given instruction, and neither mum or dad had first aid training.

Mum, being the great all-rounder she was, however, kept a well-stocked first aid box which contained bandages—crepe and cotton—sticking plasters, ointment (the wonder cure-all cream she always swore by was Valderma), lint—pink for "drawing out" infections, or white merely for protection—iodine, eye bath, a pair of sharp scissors, and of course Dettol completed the kit. Mum being mum, she must also have learned a special healthcare trick, for she kept borassic crystals to place on a warm, wet patch of pink lint to draw out any infection. A cure for a head cold was for a teaspoon of "Vick" dropped into a bowl of boiling water over which her "patient," with a towel draped over their head, inhaled the fumed steam.

A Visit from the Minister

"The minister's at the Steenie Brig! He's on his way here!"

Mum always kept a lookout when the minister was expected. Routine "home visits" by the family minister was a practice that died out sometime in the 1960s. But back in the 1950s, when the Rev. Mr John Cumming announced from the pulpit that he was to visit our area, mum and dad made special efforts to tidy up the house and we were given strict instructions to be on our best behaviour. I don't know why it was such a nervous time, but I recall hearing mum say, "He's on his way! I can see him from the window."

Looking back, I sense that it was simply that "the family" should be noted by the minister as being clean, tidy, and of respectable appearance. I was never "in the room" when the minister visited and, and I can only surmise what the topics of conversation would have been.

Home Pets

"Your tadpoles will have to go now!"

Although mum grew up on a farm, she never wished to have either a cat or dog in the house as a pet. My parents did keep, during WW2 years, bantam hens and rabbits at Annfield Cottage, Barry Road, although they never troubled themselves with such activities at Admiral Street, or at Shamrock Street. However, Peem and I looked after a pet rabbit which I confess, while appearing healthy enough, was kept in a rather restricted hutch. It was dad who took the time to ensure it was properly fed and cleaned. Sadly, this was not really a "pet-friendly" practice.

Apart from occasionally keeping goldfish, which may have been won at various carnivals (a practice now quite rightly abolished), the only other (part-time) pets I kept were tadpoles. "Pets," I suspect, is not quite the correct term! Somehow, I obtained a large glass barrel-shaped tank which I sat on my west-facing windowsill. I collected frog spawn from the burn which ran alongside the small market garden in what is now called Panbride Street. We called the stream "the ditchie," which at Panbride Street began to run underground—presumably out to the sea. I kept the water refreshed in my tank, and always took weed or water cress from the stream and kept it in the tank. I studied the developing frogs and fed the tadpoles on raw egg-white until the day mum protested, "Your tiny frogs are now jumping out of the tank! They'll have to go!"

Transport

"Dynamos are alright, but no use in ice and snow."

I have mentioned bikes elsewhere, but at this point I merely wish to add that all through my young life I graduated through the many sizes of frames. The size of the frame was measured from the top of the frame under the saddle to the centre point on the crank shaft. My progression took me from a 14 inch frame up to a 21 inch frame, with a succession of "new second-hand" bikes as my legs grew. During the 1950s, very active and comprehensive market information about second-hand bikes was published in *The Courier* under different categories—i.e. a range of ladies'/gents'/children's bikes, all listed under frame sizes—which was a valuable source for essential purchases.

The hazards of cycling during winter months through deep snow was difficult, but melted slush which froze at night was more troublesome. Being caught in a rut of ice was very dangerous. Worst of all, I think, was the unseen, lethal "black ice." This was frozen rain that looked like water and was the cause of many serious accidents and occasionally death for pedestrians, cyclists, and drivers of vehicles. Young inexperienced drivers were unsuspecting victims of black ice, especially on clear spring mornings just as light was breaking. We have improved weather warnings nowadays.

Motorcars

Until the 1950s, cars were in the main all black—with the rare exception of the occasional twin colour scheme of black and deep purple, or black and maroon. I think all petrol-driven UK models were popular until Japanese, German and French imports began to creep in from the 1970s onwards.

Buses

"A six-day return ticket, please!"

The above was my usual Monday morning request when I went to work in Dundee by bus in 1960. My early public bus experiences were always smoky and packed, forcing a bus conductress/conductor to squeeze his or her way around the bus to collect the fares. However, I have to say that timetables were closely followed. During and immediately after the Second World War, buses were few and far between, and I recall my mum's dismay when we travelled to and from Woodside Croft to see an approaching "utility" bus. This meant no cushioned seating—simply wooden slats. Conductors were used on all public buses up to the end of the 2020–21 pandemic, when Stagecoach buses, as an example, had the driver collect fares on entry, thus disposing of a cost factor. On paying the driver now, there is not even the issue of a ticket.

My Junior Permit bus pass from 1956, allowing me free travel daily to Arbroath.

Train journeys have changed drastically too. On local trains, it was normal to find a coach with twelve-seat compartments—that is, each compartment consisted of six seats facing opposite, and no toilet facility. For longer trips, corridor coaches were employed which offered small, separate compartments of three or four seats facing, and with a sliding door. On long trips the latter was preferred, as there were toilets at the end of each coach. As with buses, smoking was permitted at the time, which was unpleasant, although I'm sure there were some non-smoking compartments. Coaches were labelled 1st or 3rd class (I can't recall seeing 2nd class, nor do I know what that offered), which determined the quality of décor and seating fabric. It was possible to book seats in compartments in advance, in which case a paper ticket was posted at the booked seat(s). This worked well until you found someone sitting in your seat and they had to be asked to move—a practice that still causes some trouble to this day.

It was always of interest to note which photos or watercolour pictures were displayed in glass frames in the compartments. My impression is that it was mainly seaside resorts which were featured—and, in the main, Welsh or English towns. I recall one journey I made from London to Scotland in the late 1960s in a corridor train, when all seats were filled and passengers were standing in the entire length of the corridor. Unfortunately, I could only find a space exactly at the point where two coaches were coupled. I sat on my suitcase for very many long and extremely uncomfortable miles while the two coaches violently shook, and the noise was unbearable. I put my faith in the engineering! Nowadays coaches are open plan for the length of the coach.

Another feature now gone was that trains had a baggage coach at the end of the train. Various items were transported—anything from boxes of fresh fish and baskets of fresh raspberries to bicycles and large trunks. A guard, equipped with a whistle and red or green flags or lamps, also travelled in the last luggage coach.

Street Lighting

"Your face is a funny orange colour, Peem!"

My earliest awareness of street lighting was when the lamplighter (or "lampy") walked his patch around the town at predetermined times and, with the aid of a long pole and hook, pulled down the chain to allow a full flow of gas to light the mantle contained within the glass lamp box. This practice worked well until, in the mid-1950s, routes were electrified and all lampposts contained an electric bulb. I think the first electric lights to be installed were the tall ones in the High Street. It was quite a thrill to see ourselves so clearly at night in the unaccustomed bright light. In Carnoustie's case, the lights had an orange glow which added to our mild amusement and amazement. I recall one night on our way home from Scouts having great fun viewing each other in the orange glow—it was a ground-breaking change in our little town to have such "modern technology"—although back then we didn't even know that phrase.

I recall reading about lamplighters back in the 1880s–90s. Evidently, each "lampy" had a determined number of lamps to light but, as the town's streets developed, the Lampies put in a complaint to the Burgh Council seeking more money or for them to recruit more lamplighters to cover an expanded area. They had strict rules to light lamps by certain times, and this was at the root of the problem.

The Arbroath Baths

"A wee bag o' chips wi' brown sauce, please!"

Thursday evenings were special when Peem, Billy Coffin (Coffey) and I set off by bus to Arbroath Baths (an indoor swimming pool), where Mr Moonie—the sweetie shop man in Carnoustie—taught us to swim. A swim, a hot shower, and then change in the "open area" where boys dressed in one group. Once spruced up, with our "dooker" rolled up in a wet towel, we set off to a nearby chip shop to buy a wee bag of chips with our favourite brown sauce. Oh my goodness, what luxury that was! Then time to jump on the bus at Brothock Brig heading back to Carnoustie.

Darning, Collars and Buttons

"Now, that'll need to do 'til the end of the year!"

It's unheard of today, but in my young days footwear and clothing had to last a long time. Socks were routinely darned until they fell apart. Mum used an empty jam jar which she inserted into a sock while she darned a heel. Shirts had to be used up to the last gasp too! One way was for mum to "turn" the collar to permit longer wear. Shoes too had to enjoy a long life. Dad had a steel shoe last which sat on his knees, into which fitted a socket of differing sizes of solid steel feet. He was then able to hammer in "segs" or "tackets" into shoes and boots.

More of the Wee Things

"Just a puckle o' memories!"

It's comforting to look back at some of the small, irrelevant events in life. Some are so simple, and yet we all store key moments with great fondness. Below are a few which come to mind:

- The rippling skin on mum's speciality rice pudding as she pulled the cooking tray from the oven.

- Do you remember, for example, standing at a bus stop waiting for a bus and feeling your feet stone-cold freezing—only to get home and heat your frozen toes at the coal fire? Yes, a certainty for a chilblain or two.

- In the days when smoking was glamourised by Hollywood, it was the done thing to have a packet of ten ciggies at the ready. When Christmas time came along, a cigarette case was a posh gift for a pal and/or a packet of 50 cigarettes. Just to be extra generous, the fifty would be "full strength and tipped."

- I still have it today! What, you may ask? The hard little bulge on the middle finger of my right hand! Why is it there? Well, you, see the school-issued pens and nibs were fine, but the design was such that in tense moments during writing, the severe pressure cut into my finger. A schooldays hazard that left at least one mark with me for life!

- Remember when birds pecked the tops off milk bottles?

- And another part of history: the tax disc we had to paste on the car windscreen.

- I recall the evenings when we sat huddled around the living room fire as we watched the red glow of coal gradually disappear, and the inevitable burning pattern of legs which had been roasted—"tartan legs," as some people called them

- My mum made her own jam for many years, but she refused to use a product called "Certa." This was a product which helped the jam to thicken. She prided herself that her jam-making didn't require special "aids."

- January was a time when Seville oranges were plentiful in the shops. Housewives bought great quantities of sugar crystal to make their own marmalade.

- In the 1950s, grocery shops sold canned whole chickens—a practice that seems unthinkable in 2025.

- Hen's feet. My friends from the country areas used to bring to the school playground a severed hen's foot. The game was to pull the tendon thus making the foot work—a bit like a claw!

My Own Background

1945: Aged 4, I started school at Barry Church in August, transferring to Carnoustie Junior Secondary School in 1947.

1955: In October, I left school and started work as an apprentice radio and TV engineer.

1956: I commenced work as an apprentice grocer with Wm Low & Co. Ltd. At No.4 Dundee Street, Carnoustie.

1960: At the age of 19, I was appointed to manage a Wm Low & Co. shop at Brantwood Avenue in Dundee.

1962: I was appointed to manage a larger shop, which was designated as a "self-selection" store—a precursor to the kind of self-service store as we know them today.

1963: Aged 23, I left Wm Low & Co. and was appointed Distributive Trades Lecturer at Dundee Commercial College in the Cowgate, Dundee.

1968: After five years of teaching, I joined The Grocers' Institute in London, and was

ROBERT (BOB) MURRAY: A Scotsman from Bonnie Dundee but now lives in St. Ives, Huntingdonshire, covering the Eastern region as Training Officer. Married with one young daughter. Has been through the mill in the grocery trade having worked for a Scottish multiple organisation. Has also spent some time in teaching students studying Food Distribution.

Robbie publicised as Training Officer for the Eastern Region with the Grocers' Institute.

appointed Training Development Officer for East England.

1969: I joined Dundee wholesale grocery company "Watson & Philip" as Training Officer.

1975: I was appointed Group Personnel Manager of Watson & Philip plc., a role in which I was employed until being made redundant after 33 years of service, aged 62.

My Work History

Age 10 to 12: Paperboy for Harry Christie in High Street, Carnoustie.

Age 12 to 15: Delivery message boy for Wm Low & Co., No.4 Dundee Street, Carnoustie.

Age 15: For 6 months, Apprentice Radio/TV Engineer at Reekie's, Arbroath.

Age 15 to 19: Apprentice Grocer, Wm Low & Co., Dundee Street, Carnoustie.

Age 19 to 21: Manager for Wm Low & Co., Brantwood Avenue, Dundee.

Age 21 to 22: Manager for Wm Low &Co., Logie Street, Lochee, Dundee.

Age 22 to 23: Manager for Wm Low & Co. at Perth Road, Dundee.

Age 23 to 28: Distributive Trades Lecturer, Dundee College of Commerce.

Age 28 to 29: Training Officer, The Grocers' Institute, London

Age 29 to 54: Training Officer, Watson & Philip plc., Dundee. Later Personnel Manager, then Group Personnel Manager for 3,000 employees.

Age 54 to 62: Personnel Manager, Watson &Philip plc., Staines-upon-Thames, London, Middlesex.

All of my employment experiences above are outlined in my *Grocer's Boy* trilogy:

- *The Grocer's Boy: A Slice of his Life in 1950s Scotland*, 2018.

- *The Grocer's Boy Rides Again: Another Slice of his Life in 1960s Scotland and Beyond*, 2020.

- *The Grocer's Boy Gets Down to Business: The End Slice of his Career from the Easy going Seventies to the Ultra Competitive Nineties*, 2022.

Modern Technology

"The future will be spelt out by science and engineering—and by the tussle between communism and democracy!"

A sociology lecturer once said the above to me in the 1970s. I have often said that my generation, specifically, has had the most peaceful, safe, and fortunate time in all of history—and perhaps so good, it will be impossible to repeat in years to come.

For instance, I was never called up to fight for my country. I had a stable school experience followed by a period when jobs abounded, and my working life was assisted greatly by a well-arranged further education system. My spending power was adequate when I became a self-sufficient house owner. I found finance available, and when required I was able to buy the many modern available "white goods" such as a fridge, cooker, and washing machine.

My work career was uninterrupted, and indeed enhanced by ample opportunities. Fundamental to my comfortable ongoing existence into retirement, I found my employer's pension adequate and secure.

Political stability was also a factor in my favour—at least, up until the struggle for Scottish independence.

Radio and TV were examples of the many improvements in my lifetime and, as I write this, I look back and see how fortunate I was, and am, to enjoy a fridge/freezer, market leader vacuum cleaner, washing machine, tumble dryer, microwave, and—quite recently—an air-fryer. All of these are examples of growing science and engineering successes.

Modern house-building standards have been improved by safer practices and materials (albeit with a few national horror stories of "bad" concrete and flammable cladding). Statistics of road deaths and domestic house fires have been greatly reduced, and the range and standard of medical health services have blossomed compared to my life in the 1950s. (Sadly, as I write, new politics are at work where the positivity I enjoyed in all my previous decades is turning in some cases to despondency and negativity.)

No one before my generation had all that I had, or have, and as I write this, I sense generations after me will not have it either—changes positive and negative are ahead for my children and grandchildren. My sadness for those in the future is caused by world climatic change and the impact of all that comes with that. Additionally, the world political order is under growing stresses, namely by the tensions between "the West" and China, Iran, North Korea, Russia and other non-democratic states around the world.

Admittedly, modern freedoms, better policing, and judicial systems—and more open communications—have unearthed and exposed many wicked, unsavoury, and damaging practices which went on unheard and unseen during my lifetime. Unfortunately, there are instances where people at the top of some organisations—both private and public—have failed to act responsibly.

My constant answer when thinking of the future is that, again, the efforts of scientists and engineers will continue to improve lives. Improved microelectronics devices, improved travel, the work of drones, driverless vehicles, and the impact of AI will all have a part to play. All of the above is a far cry from the practices carried out by my father; it's a long list:

- Maintaining every aspect of the family's bicycles.

- Scraping out ashes from the fireplace every morning, and setting a new fire with paper and kindling.

- Gardening without a petrol-driven or electrically-driven lawnmower.

- Shaving only with soap and a razor.

- Handwriting every letter—no laptop, word processor, or Internet.

- Only a public phone box in which to make a call.

- Bicycle, bus or train everywhere—no car for transport.

- No electricity in the house—just gas and paraffin heaters, or a coal fire. I recall my Arbroath friend John Knox relating in a talk to the Carnoustie Probus Club that the statistics of the 1950s of deaths in

Arbroath told a horror story of the number of people falling into the harbour, being burned alive in their own armchair by smoking when drunk, and road deaths. Health and safety, often maligned, has nevertheless given us a safer world .

"Aye, I've nothin' tae complain aboot!"

The 2020s: Brexit, COVID-19, The Ukraine War, Food Banks, Warm Places, the Cost of Living and the "Employed Poor"

"Our Carnoustie world is changing in front of our eyes, Peem—and not much for the better!"

The current decade has presented many challenges, and a period of unpredictability which has affected not just Carnoustie, but every corner of the world.

Brexit

In a UK referendum on whether Britain should leave the European Union, the nation was split almost evenly. The result showed that 52% voted to remove ourselves, while the balance (48%) elected to remain. The population was divided into "remainers" and "leavers".

The EU had upset many by its vast administrative arrangements and the heavy cost. This was compounded by the many EU laws which prevented the UK parliament from exercising its own legal wishes. Some decisions relating to terrorism legal cases received high profile when the UK was prevented from applying its wishes to deport criminals. It was said by would-be "leavers" that Britain had lost its sovereignty. The issue became emotional more than economical.

Nearer home here in Carnoustie, the impact of leaving was immediately felt when the many fruit pickers had to return to their country of origin. Likewise, many employees in the National Health Service, care home industry, and transport (lorry drivers) left the country. In short, "Brexit"—as it has become known—created large-scale staff shortages and resultant cost increases. In retrospect, Brexit is now considered by some to have been a bad decision economically. Looking back, much of the campaign was whipped up on an emotional level.

COVID-19: The Coronavirus Pandemic

In 2023 and 2024, we saw the most difficult living periods in the country's recent history. I was too young to have experienced the direct impact of the Second World War. However, the general improvement in living standards and the rising cost of living were brought into sharp focus when the coronavirus pandemic struck the world.

In March 2020, the UK felt the first blow to society when "lockdown" was introduced. The impact on society in general lasted three years, with direct implications for life and work. For personal safety reasons, thousands of workers began working from home. Many thousands across the country, where permitted by their employer, still prefer to work from home. It seems likely that the pandemic has created new and permanent working arrangements for many employees.

The twin impact of Brexit and the pandemic created huge burdens on the government in financial, employment, education, and health services, with health and education in particular suffering most.

In Carnoustie, as elsewhere, space distancing in queues was introduced and services were closed.

The Russian Invasion of Ukraine

When Russia invaded Ukraine in February 2022, the UK was hit by yet another drain on the nation's reserves. The ripple effect created price and delivery problems surrounding gas and oil supplies. It was then apparent that Ukraine's inability to grow and supply its usual vast stock of grain would result in lower supplies and increased commodity prices .

Food Banks, Warm Places, Cost of Living and the "Employed Poor"

The combined effect of Brexit, COVID-19 and the Ukraine war not only had a massive negative financial impact on the nation's reserves, but the "filter down" hit the entire population in varying degrees. For example:

- Domestic gas and electricity charges almost doubled, and the government was forced to provide financial "cushions" to help every household.

- The number of families designated as being "in poverty" shot up.

- Food banks were set up all over the country.

- To help keep people comfortable, places (sometimes charity shops and church halls) became 'Warm Places,' where the poor could obtain some winter comfort.

- The term "The Employed Poor" was introduced. This described the real problem of families where both parents worked, but with the massive increases in household expenditure they had been tipped into a state of poverty.

- Part of the comfort factor for staff (as well as the reduced heating of offices) was resolved by allowing employees to avoid costly travel to work by encouraging working from home. In some cases, it caused employers to rethink working practices on a permanent basis.

Some Final Thoughts

As I sign off from my tales of yesteryear, I would like to make mention of the creation of a Heritage Group in the town.

During my year as President of Carnoustie Probus Club, I invited Kirriemuir Heritage Society to give a talk to members about the work of the Society. I was immediately struck with the idea of forming a similar group for Carnoustie.

As a starting point, I arranged to meet Mr Derek Miller—Chairman of Carnoustie Community Development Trust—to set out my intentions. The title "Friends of Carnoustie and District Heritage" was created, and I set out to gather some friends to outline my plans.

The first meeting of the Steering Group was held in October 2018, and the following members determined to create a management committee:

Margaret Bowman, Kay Landsburgh, Peter Murphy, David Ross, George Stewart, John Stirling, David Taylor, Linda Nicol, and myself.

In due course the group drafted a constitution, developed a business plan, and set out to seek funding. Following a pause caused by the COVID-19 pandemic, the inaugural AGM was held in April 2023 when a management committee comprising the following was formed: Myself as Chair, Margaret Bowman (Publicity), Linda Nicol (Speaker's Convener), John Stirling (Secretary), and David Taylor (Treasurer).

The prime aims are to hold public meetings where visiting speakers give talks on relevant heritage matters, offer reminiscence discussion groups, video record social history interviews, and create local heritage walks.

In the field north of Carnoustie High School, an extensive Neolithic site was discovered in 2018/19. The artefacts are so rare that most were sent to London History Museum and some to the National Museum in Edinburgh. Only some replicas have been displayed in Carnoustie Library.

At the time of writing public talks have been arranged for the group on the following topics:

18th September 2019: *Carnoustie and District in the 17th Century* by Norman Atkinson

20th November 2019: *The Work of Angus Archives* by Craig Pearson

10th February 2020: *The Carnoustie Hoard* by Guard Archeology

14th September 2022: *The Smieton Story* by Iain Flett

9th November 2022: *The History of the Black Watch* by Ronnie Proctor

8th February 2023: *Victims of the Tay Rail Disaster* by Murray Nicoll

14th June 2023: *History of Local Railways* by Ian Fowlis

13th September 2023: *The Jacobite Uprising* by Iain McIntosh

8th November 2023: *History of Carnoustie's British Legion* by Davie Paton

14th February 2024: *History of Panbride Church* by Linda Nicoll

12th June 2024: *History of Carnoustie Ladies Golf* (visit)

11th September 2024: *Wartime Defences of the Tay Estuary* by Margaret Bowman

13th November 2024: *Forfar Witch Trial* by Shaun Wilson

12th April 2025: *Angus Folklore* by Dr Erin Farley

Ongoing Friends of Carnoustie and District Heritage projects at the time of completing this personal heritage 'walk' through my life in Carnoustie are as follows:

- Continuing with a series of filmed "social" interviews of selected individuals in the town who will help to provide an insight into life in the 2020s.
- Development of selected heritage walks in and around the town.
- Producing selected heritage "guided tours".
- Continuing the reminiscence "Bothy Nichts" events.
- Creation of an audit or gazetteer of retail establishments and economic business activity in the town.
- Make a comprehensive record by video of the town and district.
- Develop illustrated talks relating to historic heritage places of interest.

Acknowledgements

I would like to thank my brother James "Peem" Murray, not only for his sketch but also for helping me to source some of the photos which appear in this book.

Thank you also to Tom and Julie Christie of Extremis Publishing for all of their help and advice in bringing this project to life.

I must thank the "modern day" thinking of my parents, and especially my mother for her up to date approach of taking photos of family groups all those 80 + years ago. I have to thank her for the various black and white photos contained within this book. This was achieved by the "modern technology" that was available at the time, and the equivalent of the latest iPhone or laptop of today—namely the Box Brownie camera.

This was a black box about the size of half a brick. It had to be held at waist height in the right hand with the thumb placed over the lever, ready to take a picture, while the left hand had to be cupped around the image seen on the screen at the top of the box (without cupping carefully, the photo might be spoiled). Equally, too slow a lever would over-expose, thus spoiling the photograph in a different way. Care had to be taken to get a good result, especially while inserting and removing a roll of film. I have the impression that ladies were more interested and skilled than men when it came to loading cameras and taking photos.

Can you imagine, in the 1930s and '40s, the thrill of picking up a packet of photos from a photo studio or chemist shop to view the cutting edge invention of the black and white photo?

Notes on Front Cover Artwork

Immediately beyond the first sunshade on the right is Carnoustie's Municipal Building, designed and built by Mr James Bruce in 1898–99 for the sum of £5000.

Further along on the right, at the corner of Lochty Street and High Street, is a shop with a curved doorway and a row of shops beyond. The entire block of shops and dwellings above were planned and built by Miss Bruce. On the 6th May 1910, the Town Council approved that the entire block be named "Paris Place".

Across the road on the corner of Fox Street and High Street is the Kinloch Arms Hotel, named after Mr George Kinloch—the man renowned for planning the first street plan of the town.

In the centre distance is the dome roof of a building located at "The Cross"—the town's favourite New Year celebration spot.

About the Author

Robert Taylor Murray was born in Barry, near Carnoustie, in 1940. Growing up in Westhaven and later residing in Carnoustie itself, he attended Barry and Carnoustie Schools before becoming an apprentice grocer with William Low & Company Ltd. He qualified as a Member of The Grocers' Institute, and was appointed manager of William Low's Brantwood branch in Dundee, becoming the company's youngest ever manager at the age of 19. He later oversaw the Logie Street branch in Lochee.

Robert went on to manage a larger third branch in Dundee and then, after attending further education management courses, discovered he was sufficiently qualified to successfully apply for a post as a lecturer in distributive trades subjects at Dundee Commercial College – a position he held for five years. Realising how much the retail trade was changing and feeling he was less in touch to reflect the current scene, he applied to join The Grocers' Institute and was appointed Training Development Officer for part of London and east England, where he advised companies and colleges on training in the retail grocery trade.

After two years he returned to the Dundee area when he was appointed Training Officer for Watson & Philip, a national wholesale food distributor. He remained with that company for thirty-three years, during which time he was appointed Personnel Manager and eventually became Group Personnel Manager with responsibility for three thousand employees and, latterly, in the London area.

Robbie's recollections of his early days in the grocery trade, *The Grocer's Boy*, was published by Extremis Publishing in 2018. The story continued in *The Grocer's Boy Rides Again*, published in 2020, which followed Robbie's professional development throughout the busy days and radical changes of the Swinging Sixties, and concluded with *The Grocer's Boy Gets Down to Business* in 2022, which charted his career from the seventies until the turn of the century.

Following a company acquisition he became redundant at the age of sixty-two. In retirement he has again been actively involved in amateur theatre. He frequently writes short stories and poetry.

He has authored a stage presentation on the life of Robert Burns, *The Spirit of Robbie Burns*, which has been performed several times by amateurs in Tayside. The script was published as a book by Extremis Publishing in 2019.

Robbie was elected a Fellow of the Royal Society of Arts in 2020. He has two daughters and four grandchildren. When he is not writing, he enjoys travelling, hillwalking and golfing.

Also Available from Extremis Publishing

THE GROCER'S BOY
By Robert Murray

The 1950s in Carnoustie: a beautiful seaside town on the Tayside coast, and a place which was to see rapid social and technological advancement during one of the fastest-moving periods of cultural change in recent British history.

In *The Grocer's Boy*, Robert Murray relates his account of an eventful childhood in post-War Scotland, drawing on fond memories of his loving family, his droll and often mischievous group of friends, and the many inspirational people who influenced him and helped to shape his early life.

Join Robert on his adventures in retail as he advances from his humble beginnings as a delivery boy for the famous William Low grocery firm, all the way to becoming the youngest manager in the company's history at just nineteen years of age. Read tales of his hectic, hard-working time as an apprentice grocer — sometimes humorous, occasionally nerve-wracking, but never less than entertaining.

From Robert's early romances and passion for stage performance to his long-running battle of wits with his temperamental delivery bike, *The Grocer's Boy* is a story of charm and nostalgia; the celebration of a happy youth in a distinctive bygone age.

Also Available from Extremis Publishing

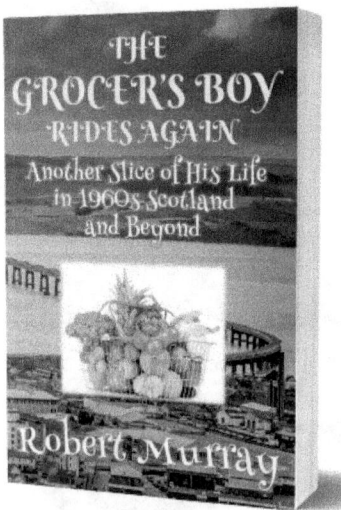

THE GROCER'S BOY RIDES AGAIN
By Robert Murray

When the Swinging Sixties arrived in Tayside, Robert Murray had just become the youngest manager in the history of famous grocery business William Low & Co. Ltd. at only nineteen years of age. Little could he have realised that this was to be just the beginning of a decade of incredible social and cultural change for Scotland and the wider world—a revolution which would touch every life and workplace.

In this sequel to his much-loved book *The Grocer's Boy*, Robert discusses the trials and tribulations of being a traditional grocer at the dawn of the supermarket age, before moving on to new challenges later in the decade which included an eventful tenure in the fast-moving domain of college education and a step further afield into the busy corporate world.

Recounting his loving family ties and enduring friendships, marriage and parenthood, nostalgic reminiscence and thoughtful reflection, *The Grocer's Boy Rides Again* takes a fresh look at this most iconic of decades, considering a country which was in a period of rapid transition but where a helpful attitude and good customer service remained of paramount importance.

Also Available from Extremis Publishing

THE GROCER'S BOY GETS DOWN TO BUSINESS
By Robert Murray

What happens when a grocer's boy moves from the saddle of his delivery bike to an executive's chair? As the 1970s dawned, Robert Murray was on the way up—newly appointed to a senior role in one of Scotland's most respected grocery distribution businesses. However, fate would have more than a few surprises in store for the man who had worked his way up from humble beginnings in grocery delivery on rural Tayside to the top level of corporate decision-making.

But it wasn't all about the company boardroom; Robert's life was full of incidents and surprises during these unpredictable decades of his career, which saw his young family grow and new friendships forged. Time and again, he discovered that the importance of professional camaraderie was just as vital as meeting the needs of the increasingly-demanding consumer.

From the social and economic turbulence of the 1980s to the ruthless commercial competitiveness of the 1990s, Robert witnessed sweeping changes in the grocery world—a distributive trades revolution which was to transform the way companies did business in the UK and far beyond. Join him as he pedals on through thirty years in the grocery trade before parking up his old pushbike for the final time.

Also Available from Extremis Publishing

THE SPIRIT OF ROBBIE BURNS
By Robert Murray

The whole world knows the legend that is Scotland's national bard, Robert Burns. But what was the story behind the meteoric success of this literary genius, whose works are still performed and enjoyed to this very day?

Appearing in print for the first time, Robert Murray's acclaimed stage play follows the life of Burns from his formative years in Ayr through to his success and celebrity in Edinburgh and later farming life in Dumfries. You will meet his friends, learn of his inspirations, and discover intimate details of his many romantic encounters.

Related with warm wit and keen insight, *The Spirit of Robbie Burns* delves into the life of one of Scotland's most complex and colourful characters to explore his timeless work and the world he lived in. The text of the play is accompanied by performance notes and detailed appendices, which will make it an essential addition to any good Burns Night celebration.

For details of new and forthcoming books from Extremis Publishing, including our monthly podcasts, please visit our official website at:

www.extremispublishing.com

or follow us on social media at:

www.facebook.com/extremispublishing

www.linkedin.com/company/extremis-publishing-ltd-/

www.ingramcontent.com/pod-product-compliance
Lightning Source LLC
Chambersburg PA
CBHW060538010526
44119CB00052B/747